THE WORLD OF
SAILING

THE WORLD OF
SAILING

MARTIN HEDGES

ELSEVIER-DUTTON PUBLISHING CO INC
NEW YORK

Published by Elsevier-Dutton Publishing Co. Inc.,
2, Park Avenue, New York, N.Y. 10016.

Produced by Basinghall Books Limited,
59, Cambridge Road, Kings Heath, Birmingham.

Designed by Roy Williams.

Edited by Janet MacLennan.

Picture research by Mark and Marisa Heseltine.

ISBN: 0-525-70725-5.

Library of Congress Catalogue No: 80-65587.

Printed in Hong Kong
by South China Printing Co.

1 THE CHALLENGE   6
2 SAILING THEORY   20
3 THE BOAT   30
4 RIGGING   42
5 SAILING SAFE   58
6 CAST OFF   76
7 CAPSIZING AND AFTER   100
8 IN TUNE   114
9 GETTING YOUR BEARINGS   126
10 WEATHER   144
11 FOUL WEATHER   156
12 A 'NOBLE PRACTICAL ART'   166
13 LAYING UP   172
14 BUYING A BOAT   180
INDEX   190

The successful British Admiral's Cup boat, *Marionette*, beats to windward in a moderate breeze.

1 THE CHALLENGE

A brisk thrash to windward in crowded waters demands continued concentration from the crew.

7

There can be few of us who have not experienced the lure of the sea. The crowds which throng beaches all over the world are evidence enough of the attractions of the waves. For some it is enough just to watch them roll to the shore or crash against cliffs but for others fulfilment can only come from venturing onto the waves to meet the challenge they afford.

Ever since man was placed on earth water has presented him with a challenge. It is there to be used, to be contained and to be crossed. At first it was to be crossed in search of new territories and new hunting grounds but as man developed so did his desire for possessions and his need for more lands. In search of these he needed a means of transport – for he still had not invented the wheel – and there was the moving water in rivers and seas to carry him.

When it was that man first set sail may never be known but it can only have been a short step from his use of paddles to propel and guide him to his realization that the wind could help to carry him. Certainly a ship with sails is clearly visible on a painted Egyptian vase dated 3200–2900BC but it is likely that even then the sail had been in use for thousands of years.

At first the sail was used as an auxiliary means of propulsion in conjunction with paddles or oars, as in Roman galleys and Viking longships. The earliest sails were square rigged, hanging from a yard which, in turn, was suspended from the mast at its center point. Because of the limitations of movement in the yard, the sail could only propel the ship forward when the wind was behind it. (The term square rigged, incidentally, does not mean that the sails have four equal sides but that they are 'set square' – at right angles – to the mast.)

The alternative was to devise a sail which would be effective no matter on which side of it the wind blew: the fore-and-aft sail. This is hung on a hinge behind the mast so that it is free to swing from side to side to take advantage of wind from any and every direction. The shape of such a sail, known as a *lateen*, can be four-sided or triangular.

In the Middle Ages these two kinds of rig were used together on the great three-masted ships which set forth on their voyages of discovery to open the oceans to the Western world. A typical example was the *Mayflower*, which carried the Pilgrim Fathers across the Atlantic from England to America in the 17th century. She was a relatively small three-masted ship which could carry seven sails, including a lateen which was set on the mizzen mast – that is, the mast nearest the aft of the ship – and six square-rigged sails.

This combination of sails continued to be used on the great ocean-going ships in war and peace even into the 19th century and can still be seen today on the famous training ships which, though

Participants in the 1974 Tall Ships' Race. These splendid vessels provide unique opportunities of adventure and team training for young people throughout the world. Here *Amerigo Vespucci, Tovarishch, Dar Pomorza* and *Kruzenshtern* reflect the international character of this popular event.

Traditional rigs are increasingly popular with the romantic element today.

Old boats like this can still get up and go when the wind is in the right quarter.

THE CHALLENGE

Foreground:
A beautiful sailing smack.
Background:
Tall Ships which provide
interest and enjoyment for
thousands of young people in
the world wide training
movement.

basically fore-and-aft rigged, carry some elements of square rigging. It is, in fact, the square rigging on these beautiful ships which require the young sailors manning it to shin up the masts to work aloft.

While the three-masted ships continued to ply the oceans, the fore-and-aft rig was used increasingly by inshore seamen such as the fishermen and traders who plied their way between ports along their native coasts. Because the fore-and-aft sails could be controlled from deck level and responded quickly to changes in wind or of setting they were obviously favored for use on ships with small crews and also for ships which were sailing on confined waters.

At the time when steam power began to take over from sail, yachting started to become fashionable and the working ships gave way to increasingly sleek and luxurious yachts which, at first, were modelled on the small cutters and supply boats used by the last navies to retain sail.

As well as being status symbols the yachts became racing vessels: where sail had been used to carry opposing navies into war it was now to become the 'weapon' of rivals competing on a more friendly basis in races over ever-longer distances.

Such a contest was that which brought into being the famous America's Cup races which have been held over the years since 1851. It was in that year that Britain issued a challenge from the Royal Yacht Squadron at Cowes to the United States of America for a race from Cowes round the Isle of Wight. Despite the fact that Britain entered 14 boats and the only American entry was the New York Yacht Club's schooner *America*, the United States took the 100-guinea vase comfortably, finishing some eight minutes ahead of the nearest British yacht.

The vase was presented for international competition and, named after that first winning boat, the America's Cup was first put up for competition in 1857.

The *America* was startlingly different in design to the British yachts which, until this challenger from across the Atlantic won the vase in 1851, had been considered the finest in the world both in appearance and performance. The 170-ton schooner *America* was based on the design of a pilot boat. She had a low, sleek hull with steeply raked bow and stern. Her two masts were raked back at an almost alarming angle and her schooner rig had rigging which to sophisticated British eyes seemed almost laughably simple.

No challenge was made for the America's Cup until 1870, when the United States again won, to begin a sequence of success which has remained unbroken. In 1962 the first Australian challenge was issued by the Royal Sydney Yacht Squadron, which entered the sloop *Gretel*, the first Australian-designed and built 12-Meter yacht. The boat was

pitted against the American 12-Meter, *Weatherly* off Newport, Rhode Island and became the first challenger since 1934 to win even one race. *Gretel* won the second of the six races in the competition and only lost the fourth by 26 seconds. However she lost the fifth and sixth races.

In 1964 Britain issued her first challenge since 1958, when *Sceptre* had been ingloriously beaten in four straight races by *Columbia*, designed by the Madison Avenue firm, Sparkman & Stephens. The challenge this time came from the Royal Thames Yacht Club's *Sovereign*, a new boat which had been built after the designers had received help from the model-testing tank in New Jersey, USA, and which showed the American influence in her lines. Even so, the new design was to no avail and the American defender, *Constellation*, won all four races including one by as much as 20 minutes 24 seconds.

Australia returned to the fight in 1967 with *Dame Patie*, which was easily beaten by *Intrepid*, another Sparkman & Stephens design which was destined to become one of the world's most successful 12-Meter class boats.

In 1970 Australia again challenged. To mark the centenary of the first America's Cup race, the rules were altered to allow more than one challenger to come forward, the eventual entrant to be decided by selection trials. A French challenge was made by *France* but the Australian *Gretel II* was selected, only to lose to *Intrepid*.

The fourth Australian challenge was made in 1974, when the rules were altered to allow the boats to be built of aluminium. Taking advantage of this change, the Australians entered the aluminum-hulled *Southern Cross*, for which there were high hopes. The French again put up *France* as their potential challenger but *Southern Cross* won the trials convincingly, thereby further raising Australian spirits.

Meanwhile the Americans, with the biggest fleet of 12-Meter boats in the world, were also holding trials between the seemingly invincible *Intrepid* and the new *Courageous*. It was the latter which won selection and went on to maintain America's unbroken run of victories by beating *Southern Cross*.

While British designers could still not come up with either a design or the financial backing to make a challenge really feasible, Australia was again on the Rhode Island start line in 1977 with the 12-Meter, *Australia*, designed by Johan Valentin. It was significant that, again, the challenger showed signs of the American influence. In fact her designer had worked for Sparkman & Stephens.

Experts agreed that *Australia* was undoubtedly a superbly built boat and there was a strong feeling that this yacht, weighing just 54,700lbs (24.7 tonnes) and with very fine lines, would wrest the cup from the considerably heavier *Courageous*, which had narrowly won her selection trials. Again the French challenged with *France I* and *France II* but the former lost all four selection trials to *Australia*. Sweden entered *Sverige* and the Sparkman & Stephens 12-Meter *Columbia* which had been built for the 1958 event.

From all the trial races *Australia* emerged the clear choice to be set against *Courageous*, but she lost in the first race by just 108 seconds. In the next the defender's winning margin was reduced still further to only 68 seconds, but in the third race *Courageous*, which was skippered throughout by Ted Turner, a flamboyant millionaire, was two minutes and 30 seconds ahead. The fourth and final race again went to the American yacht, this time by two minutes and 25 seconds.

In the 1980 America's Cup Britain entered her first challenger since 1964, *Lionheart*, a 12-Meter weighing 30 tons and costing some £650,000. She proved a disappointment in the preliminaries, in which the other challengers were *France III*, *Australia* and *Sverige*. It was *Australia* which emerged the clear winner to challenge America's *Enterprise*. In the five races the challenger won only once – in the third race by just 28 seconds – while *Enterprise* won three times by the convincing margins of one minute 52 seconds, three minutes 48 seconds and three minutes 38 seconds, and once by a mere boat's length.

Here it has to be admitted that the place of the America's Cup in the world of sailing is by no means as well defined as it once was. At one time there could be no doubting that the chance of winning the Cup acted as a spur to designers. The yachts they built incorporated new features which, apart from being of benefit to the craft itself, could be applied virtually throughout the world of yachting. The Cup could, therefore, be claimed to be the harbinger of boat technology.

Undoubtedly the challenge and the excitement are still there but as costs have escalated the world of yachting in this class has shrunk. Innovations in design are generally confined in their application to just the one type of boat and to a limited number of sailors who can afford them.

Almost without exception it can now be said that the advancement of boat technology lies in the hands of those who design and build for the vast fraternity of small sailing racers.

Broadly speaking, what has happened in the last half of the 20th century has been a refinement of the technologies and traditions of the great days of the 'tall' sailing ships coupled with the birth of a new technology bred out of the demand for little boats which can be sailed by just one or two people. The heavy block and tackle, the giant sails and thick lines have given place to lightweight sailing boats equipped with 'furniture' which is simple, efficient and durable.

The latest British challenger for the America's Cup, *Lionheart*, receives a scrubdown.

Where once the challenge of the water was taken up by great ships manned by large crews sailing the seas, today it is accepted by men and women who venture forth in ones and twos.

It is with this ever-growing world of small sailing boats that we shall be principally concerned in the following chapters, remembering that without it there would soon be no one left to accept the challenges of the great ocean races or the single-handed adventures. Apart from giving pleasure and excitement to many thousands of enthusiasts throughout the world, small-boat sailing is the starting point, the training ground for those who would go on to bigger things.

Top left:
Running under spinnaker in heavy weather can lead to feelings of insecurity.

Left:
The modern hull can be driven easily to windward even in a blow.

Top:
The Replica yacht *America* pictured at anchor off Cowes I.O.W. during her first visit to UK waters.

It was here that the original *America* won the first challenge. The America's Cup was named after it and it is still in American hands.

Above:
The British yacht *Battlecry* and the Argentinian boat *Red Rock* fly spinnakers and bloopers during a race in the Admiral's Cup series.

Top:
A close reach under spinnaker overpresses this boat. The foredeck hand prepares the *Genoa* for rehoisting. This foresail will be less powerful but more efficient.

Left:
Clare Francis sails her *ADC Accutrac* in the Whitbread Round the World race in 1977/8.

Above:
Freedom hauls down sail after winning the third race.

Freedom leads *Australia* at the start of the first America's Cup race. *Freedom* went on to win by a convincing margin.

The ultimate in small sailboat racing; Flying Dutchmen, the larger of the Olympic two-man boats, race at Whitstable.

2 SAILING THEORY

Planing on a fast spinnaker reach.

Whether we are talking about great sailing ships or small sailing boats, the theory of how and why a boat equipped with sails moves in the water remains the same. It is a theory which needs to be understood if ever one is to become more than a mere hit-and-miss sailor – hit the bank and miss the buoy.

It is true to say that sailing is both an art and a science: certainly there is science in the creation of a successful boat through theoretical calculations, tests in wind tunnels and water tanks, in equations of aerodynamics and hydrodynamics and much more besides. Certainly, too, there is an art in getting the best out of the boat, in the intuitive understanding of a craft's characteristics and in knowing exactly the right moment to make a particular maneuver or hoist a different sail. Yet art and science together will come to nought without knowledge of the basic theory.

There are just two things which make a boat sail – air and water. Experienced sailors know and beginners will quickly find out that whether the boat sails well or badly depends on many other things too, but it is the behavior of the air and the water and their interaction on the boat – that is to say, on the hull and sails – upon which the act of sailing depends entirely.

Man's first attempts at sailing involved him in hoisting a 'sail' of some sort – quite possibly matted greenery – at right angles to the wind, which would then blow his craft along. It did not take him long to discover that with a fixed 'sail' he would only travel in the direction the wind was blowing. However, he found, too, that if he pivoted the sail on the mast he could swing it at an angle to the wind and gain some degree of alteration in his course. Even so, he could still do no more with this type of sail than sail *before the wind* that is, with the wind blowing from a point somewhere in an arc defined between about four o'clock and eight o'clock behind him. Even by using his rudder to steer, he could do nothing about sailing into the wind: hence the combined use of sail and oars – the sail to propel him when the wind was in the right quarter, the oars to use when it was not and the sail had to be lowered.

What was he to do to overcome the problem? He had to learn to appreciate two types of wind – *true wind* and *apparent wind*. True wind is the sort of wind we experience when standing still, for example, on a headland, and it was this wind which the first sailors were using to propel those early sailing boats.

However, as the boat moves, another wind can be felt: that created by the movement itself. This can best be appreciated by imagining a cyclist riding on a windless day through stationary air. The wind of his own speed will blow through his hair and across his face, yet there is no *true wind* blowing. The combination of the wind created by movement and nature's own true wind is known as the *apparent wind*, which has a direction and speed which differs from that of the true wind. It is this apparent wind which must be taken into account when determining the maneuvers of a boat.

When the wind encounters a sail it is deflected by that sail which exerts a force in the wind equal and opposite to the force exerted by the wind on the sail. The wind striking the sail on the wind-

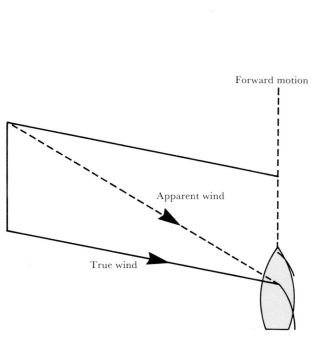

Forward motion

Apparent wind

True wind

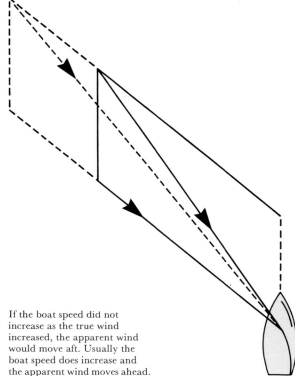

If the boat speed did not increase as the true wind increased, the apparent wind would move aft. Usually the boat speed does increase and the apparent wind moves ahead.

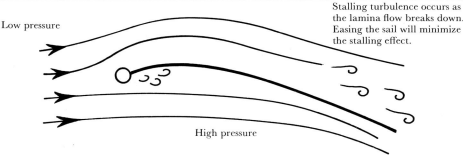

ward side is forced to change direction to avoid the obstacle. In doing so its streams of air are compressed, creating a 'corridor' of high pressure. However, on the leeward side – away from the wind – the air which had been running straight until the obstacle was encountered is drawn in behind the sail to fill what would otherwise become a vacuum. Because this air is filling a wider space than it had previously occupied, its pressure is lower and a forward suction on the sail is created.

The displacement of the air creates an *aerodynamic force* which varies in direct proportion to the surface area of the sail. It is also proportional to the mathematical square of the wind speed (that is, when the wind speed doubles the aerodynamic force quadruples). In fact the low-pressure area on the leeward side of the sail is of greater importance in terms of aerodynamic force than the high pressure area on the windward side.

Nature is nothing if not perverse and having established our theory of aerodynamic force it would seem natural that the law of equal and opposite reaction between wind and sail would mean that to get the best results you should use the sail to deflect the wind through the greatest possible angle. That, however, is not the case.

Certainly, as the sail is sheeted in to bring it closer to the wind direction, the aerodynamic force does increase – but only to a certain angle of incidence. Beyond that point the force decreases sharply. The reason for this is that the wind can deflect smoothly around the obstructive sail set at a low angle of incidence (when it is said to have *laminar flow*) but as that angle increases the smooth flow round to the leeward side is interrupted and develops into a series of rushes and swirls. Turbulence is created by the wind hitting the sail head on, bouncing off and, in effect, rushing to find its way round the sail in a series of pockets and eddies which destroy the pattern of the areas of high and low pressure.

The result is that at a critical angle of incidence (about 25 degrees) the sail stalls and must be eased beyond the critical point to allow the turbulence to cease and the correct pressures to re-establish themselves. First the sail will flap ineffectually, then it will fill to take up its correct concave shape; the crisis is over.

What of the other essential – water? Its behavior and that of the boat in it are as important as the wind and are similar in many ways. For example, a keel or a centerboard in the water behaves like a sail in the wind, with the difference that in the first case the surface is moving through the liquid while in the latter the wind is moving over the sail. However, the interactions are the same.

A boat makes *leeway* when it moves sideways or not directly forward in the water. To resist this the body of the boat underwater must present lateral resistance. This is achieved by the keel or centerboard resisting the water at what is known as the angle of leeway, setting up a reactive force perpendicular to its surface. The similarity between wind and water continues in that the lateral resistance is proportional to the surface of the keel and to the square of the boat's speed. If the water flow is laminar, the greater the angle of leeway, the higher the resistance but, as with the sail, there is a critical angle beyond which there is a stall, all thrust is lost and eddies are created in the water around the keel.

The body of the boat must have fine lines to present as little resistance as possible to encourage forward motion and it must resist heeling over by means of the design and shape and the influence of the ballast. Essentially, the larger the hull and the lower the center of gravity, the greater the resistance to heeling – and therefore the greater the inherent stability of the boat.

Two equal forces working in opposite directions act to create the *righting couple* which provides stability: the weight of the boat acting downwards through the center of gravity and the buoyant lift (*hydrostatic pressure*) acting upwards through the center of buoyancy.

A keel boat, or small sailboat with centerboard, floating on calm water without wind should be on an even keel with the center of gravity directly below the center of buoyancy. A wind from port (left) will exert a heeling force tending to tip the boat over to the right. Immediately the center of buoyancy shifts to the side to which the boat is heeling to counteract the heeling force and establish the righting couple. An increase in the weight

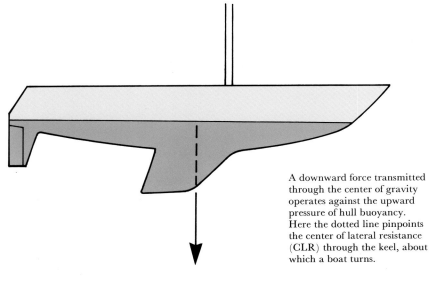

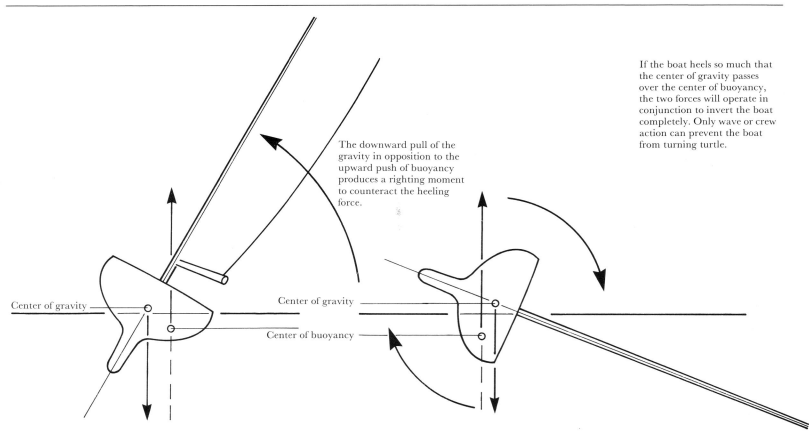

The downward pull of the gravity in opposition to the upward push of buoyancy produces a righting moment to counteract the heeling force.

Center of gravity

Center of gravity

Center of buoyancy

If the boat heels so much that the center of gravity passes over the center of buoyancy, the two forces will operate in conjunction to invert the boat completely. Only wave or crew action can prevent the boat from turning turtle.

Center of gravity

of ballast at the lowest point of lateral resistance (the fin or bulb keel), or in small sailboats, by the movable ballast (the crew) sitting as far out as possible, increases the effect of the righting couple.

There is, of course, a point beyond which the righting couple cannot increase in proportion to the degree of heel and when that angle is exceeded a capsize becomes inevitable.

With a keel boat the effectiveness of the righting couple depends largely on the shape of the hull and the placing of all weight as low as possible, leaving the deck as clear as is practical. In fact, heeling is not only inevitable but desirable so far as keel boats are concerned and they are designed to sail well when heeling. With a small sailboat, however, the righting couple is at its most effective when the boat is on an even keel and the crew's ability to move about to achieve this happy state therefore becomes important in gaining the best performance from the boat.

When a boat, or anything else, floats in water it displaces an amount of water; the weight of a boat is therefore called its *displacement*. The amount of the boat which is actually in the water, the *immersed volume*, depends upon its weight. Everything on the boat which is under the water is on the *bottom* of the boat and everything above the waterline is *topsides*.

A boat sitting in the water not unnaturally meets some resistance when it moves. This is caused by the bulk of the hull meeting the surrounding bulk of water and attempting to push it aside. Obviously the resistance will be lessened by smoothing the surface of the hull and by shaping it so that it will cut into the water cleanly,

causing as little disturbance as possible. If you hold a knife blade downwards in water and move the blade forwards with its face broad on to the direction of movement you will not only feel the considerable resistance; you will also see that in forcing it forward, eddies and whirls are created outwards. If, however, you move the knife forward with its cutting surface heading into the water it will slice through the water meeting little resistance and creating virtually no disturbance.

To a degree, this is the essence of boat design – though an over-simplification for it implies that the perfect boat's hull would be designed like a knife blade with a mast perched upon it! Apart from the need for deck space there is the requirement for a boat to have a beam – a width – to provide stability and the basis through which the righting couple and other forces can operate. There are any number of permutations that can be worked in boat design, as can be evidenced by a look at the wide variety of classes of smaller sailboats to be seen at any sailing center. All kinds of factors and needs are taken into account in the course of designing a boat. One craft may be considered 'beamy,' that is broad and rather flat, while another is deep and narrow; one may have a broad, rounded bow while another is raked and sharp. Some boats, no matter what their designers may have intended, just cannot achieve a good thrust and will not handle well.

One cause for lack of thrust which can be clearly identified (while others remain a mystery) is *drag* caused by friction between the surface of the hull and the water. The hull will be moving at a different speed to the water with which it is in

immediate contact. If we think of the water as being in layers, that layer which is nearest to the boat will find that the hull wants to pull it along with the boat. The next layer of water will wish to continue in its original direction and puts up a resistance to any change. There is, therefore, drag between hull and water and also between water and water. Further, if the hull is rough or dirty it will drag more water along with it than would a clean, highly polished hull. The result is that the layer of water being pulled in the direction of the boat is thicker, heavier and not only drags back more on the hull but also creates more disturbance in the water around. It follows that the greater the area of boat which is in the water, known as the *wetted area*, the greater the friction between hull and water. The basic 'cures' call for the designer to reduce the wetted area and to construct it from a material which offers as little resistance to the water as possible; and for the bottom to be kept as highly polished as possible.

A further form of drag also becomes apparent when a boat moves through the water: wave drag. Much as the air meeting a sail is compressed, diverted and then closes in behind the sail, so the water is cleft by the bow and closes in at the stern. In the process a series of waves is created, irrespective of whether the boat is sailing inland or on sea waves. These waves can use up much of the boat's forward propulsive energy, creating drag.

The first wave created by the boat is usually just aft of (behind) the bow but as the speed of the boat increases, so the distance between the waves becomes longer. When the second wave after the bow reaches the after end of the craft, the boat is said to have attained her critical speed. If speed

increases still more, the wave comes further behind the stern of the boat and causes turbulence which severely reduces the thrust of the boat by creating more drag.

However, a small sailboat with a fairly flat bottom has a different set of operating rules. When it reaches its critical speed it benefits from a lifting force which enables it to 'skip' or *plane* over the water. What happens is that the boat leaves its stern wave behind and lifts its bow so much that the bow wave does not form until about amidships. In this attitude the boat meets much less resistance since the wetted area is reduced to a minimum. It is thus able to reach high speeds. It follows that the ability to take advantage of conditions in which the boat will plane can be of considerable benefit to a competitor in a race.

There are other forms of friction on the hull of a boat which will affect its speed: *skin friction* and *impact friction*. The first of these arises when a thick 'skin' of water adheres to the whole of the wetted area causing the type of drag already discussed. The second occurs when the boat becomes 'out of tune' with the body of water through which it is moving because of the wave pattern in relation to

Opposite:
In marginal planing conditions the helmsman must look to exploit every wave to the best advantage.

Left:
A 505 in the 1976 European Championships held in Hayling Bay and sponsored by Dunhill.

Bottom:
Solings run under spinnakers in hot pursuit of the distant race leaders.

the weight and speed of the boat. A heavier boat is less likely to be raised sufficiently in the water for it to be affected by a series of short waves hitting the bottom with the resounding 'thwack' which characterizes this condition. A light small-sailing boat, though more prone to impact friction or resistance is able to accelerate more quickly than a longer, heavier keel boat and can reach a speed to recover much sooner.

So far we have looked at the various forces which work upon the sails and the hull. There is another, manmade force which plays an important part in the way a boat behaves: the rudder.

The sole purpose of the rudder or tiller is often considered to be to turn the boat. In fact, it has a more important function: to keep the boat on a steady course despite the contrary efforts of wind or water. The rudder makes use of the water to create a force by setting up a resistance to the liquid. The force which results is proportional to the area of the rudder blade and the square of the speed of the water (note the similarity of the formula to that for wind on sail). In addition, the force is proportional to the angle of incidence of the rudder to the laminar flow (the direction of movement through the water) and increases as that angle increases.

If the boat is moving forward and the rudder is put to port (left) the pressure is exerted on the starboard (right) face of the rudder blade, the stern of the boat is pushed to the left and so the bow swings right.

However, the rudder also exerts a braking force on the forward motion of the boat and this in-

This Phantom sailboat's severe pitching will bring its windward progress almost to a halt.

creases with the angle of incidence. If the rudder is used to excess at the start of a turn and put over too far, the braking force will be more than the turning force and a stall is likely. When a turn is about half complete it is possible to push the rudder further over because the maneuver has lessened the angle of incidence between the rudder blade and the laminar flow and the critical stalling point has been passed.

The caution against excessive movement of the rudder at the start of a turn applies also to the movement once the turn has been accomplished since the blade again must pass through the critical point of the angle of incidence. If the movement is done gently the rudder will pass through that point without causing turbulence or undue braking.

From all that has been said in this chapter it will have become obvious that to make a boat perform well requires a careful balancing act between the various forces mentioned. If any of the forces are unbalanced the boat will either *bear away* (that is, it will turn away from the most effective use of the wind) or *luff* against the helmsman's wishes (head closer into the wind than intended). When the boat tends to bear away it means that the hydrodynamic force on the leeward (the down-wind side) is greater than the aerodynamic force and the boat is said to have a *lee helm*. If the aerodynamic force is greater, the boat has a *weather helm*.

The various forces have different points through which they act. The aerodynamic force may be taken as acting through the *center of effort* or CE

and the hydrodynamic force through the *center of lateral resistance* (CLR). The position of the CE varies according to a number of factors such as the course being sailed, the position, shape and surface area of the sails and the angle at which the boat is heeled.

On the other hand the CLR alters with the speed of the boat: the greater the speed, the further forward the CLR moves. It is also changed by use of the centerboard. If the board is fully down the CLR will be forward; if it is lifted slightly, the CLR moves aft following the direction in which the board moves on its pivot. As soon as a boat has cast off and is under way the crew should endeavor to establish the correct balance between the CLR and the CE so that the craft is most likely to achieve its best speed.

Another Phantom bears away to surf down a wave – too aggressive use of the tiller slows the boat and can stall the rudder.

Keith Musto's immaculate Flying Dutchman, one of the most complex small sailing boats.

3 THE BOAT

A 505 being worked carefully to windward in moderate conditions.

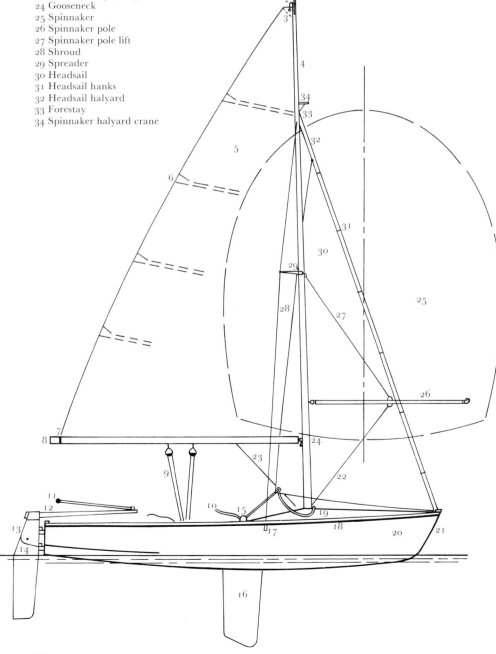

Centerboard sailboats

1 Burgee
2 Main halyard
3 Headboard
4 Mast
5 Mainsail
6 Sail batten
7 Boom black band
8 Boom
9 Mainsheet
10 Headsail sheet
11 Tiller extension (hiking stick)
12 Tiller
13 Rudder stock
14 Rudder blade
15 Headsail sheet fairlead
16 Centerboard
17 Shroud plate
18 Gunwale rubbing strip
19 Foredeck
20 Bow (starboard)
21 Stem
22 Spinnaker pole downhaul
23 Kicking strap (vang)
24 Gooseneck
25 Spinnaker
26 Spinnaker pole
27 Spinnaker pole lift
28 Shroud
29 Spreader
30 Headsail
31 Headsail hanks
32 Headsail halyard
33 Forestay
34 Spinnaker halyard crane

In this chapter we shall be looking in detail at the basic equipment of the smaller racing sailboat and the purpose for which each part is intended. Lest any reader should think that this is an unnecessary occupation, let him go to his nearest sailing club and discover just how many of its members do not know the names of the different parts of their boats. It is a safe bet that they will not be among the club's most successful sailors.

Just as it is perfectly possible for a motorist to get along well enough without knowing anything about the parts of the engine it *is* possible to sail a boat without knowing much about its component parts – but with limited success. The car will carry on happily enough so long as it has fuel, is steered properly and the gears are changed successfully and as long as no mechanical fault develops. But a boat requires a far more personal touch and more frequent attentions which will obviously not be fully paid if the helmsman or crew have not got the faintest notion of the purposes and names of the various parts.

Since it is the most noticeable part, let us start with the mast. This will have been positioned by the designer on the fore-and-aft center line of the boat at the point which, his calculations and experience tell him, will give the craft a very slight weather helm when correctly trimmed on a close-hauled course. (That course is the one which heads the boat close into the wind.) The mast is set in the mast step, which is a recess or socket in the boat's keelson (inner floor) or in a block which is itself recessed. When the mast is raised it is said to be 'stepped.'

At the head (top) of the mast is a burgee or wind vane which swings on a pivot and is counter-balanced. The purpose of the burgee is not merely decorative; it will often bear the identification of the boat's owner, club or class and the direction in which it points is that in which the apparent wind is blowing.

Below the burgee on the mast itself is a sheave, a wheel in a block, through which the main halyard is run. This is the line which is attached to the head of the mainsail and used to hoist the sail to the top of the mast. Once the mainsail is hoisted this halyard is fastened to the main halyard cleat just above the foot of the mast. The cleat is normally a wood, metal or strong plastic fitting to which the rope is attached in such a way that it is held fast yet can be released quickly in case of emergency (further reference to these will be made later).

Further down the mast is the fitting to accept another sheave; this one is for hoisting a spinnaker – a large sail which can be seen ballooning out forward and to one side of the mainsail. A little way below this sheave is the fitting for the shrouds, forestay and trapeze. The shrouds are wire ropes which are attached to the sides of the boat and are used to support the mast by adjusting each of them to the correct tension using bottle-screws. The forestay serves a similar purpose, running to the bow, where it is attached to a shackle. The trapeze wires are used to support the crew when leaning outboard of the boat.

Moving still further down the mast, there is the pivoted joint for the crosstrees. These, also known as spreaders, are literally used to spread the shroud wires apart. Considerably lower down the mast is the fitting for the spinnaker boom; this is a stay which is used to spread the foot of the spinnaker sail so that it has the best opportunity of ballooning out to its maximum surface area.

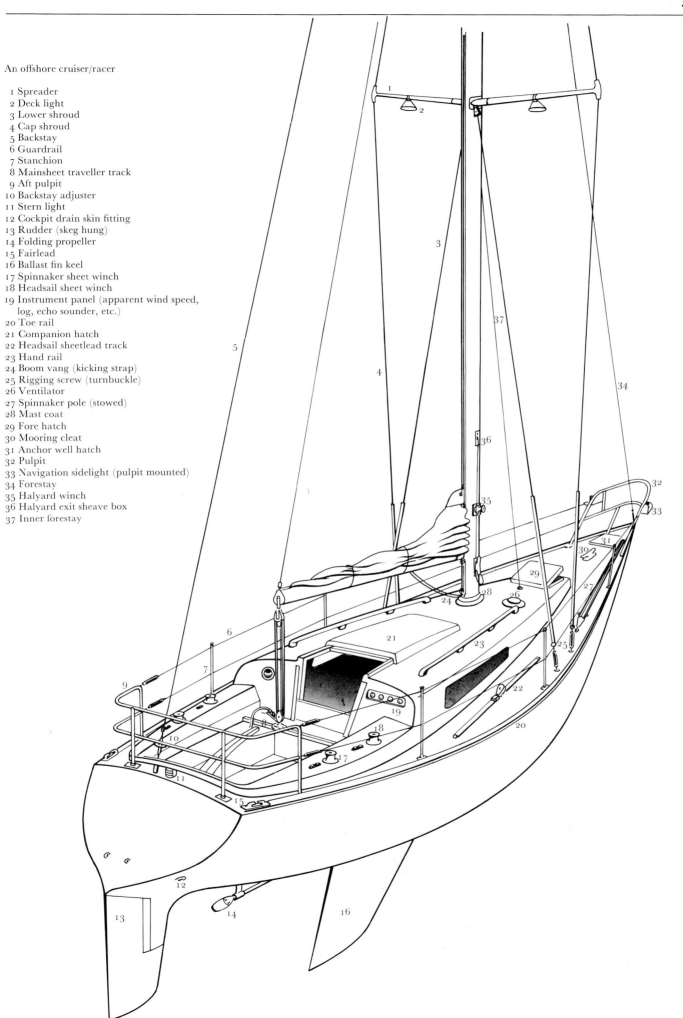

An offshore cruiser/racer

1 Spreader
2 Deck light
3 Lower shroud
4 Cap shroud
5 Backstay
6 Guardrail
7 Stanchion
8 Mainsheet traveller track
9 Aft pulpit
10 Backstay adjuster
11 Stern light
12 Cockpit drain skin fitting
13 Rudder (skeg hung)
14 Folding propeller
15 Fairlead
16 Ballast fin keel
17 Spinnaker sheet winch
18 Headsail sheet winch
19 Instrument panel (apparent wind speed,
   log, echo sounder, etc.)
20 Toe rail
21 Companion hatch
22 Headsail sheetlead track
23 Hand rail
24 Boom vang (kicking strap)
25 Rigging screw (turnbuckle)
26 Ventilator
27 Spinnaker pole (stowed)
28 Mast coat
29 Fore hatch
30 Mooring cleat
31 Anchor well hatch
32 Pulpit
33 Navigation sidelight (pulpit mounted)
34 Forestay
35 Halyard winch
36 Halyard exit sheave box
37 Inner forestay

On the aft curve of the mast is the gooseneck fitting into which the boom slots or on which it swings. The boom itself is the spar used to extend the foot of the mainsail, where it is fastened by a clew outhaul, the clew being the lower aft corner of the sail. Increasingly in modern small sailboats, the foot of the sail is fitted into a runner fastened to the top of the boom. Similarly, the forward edge of the mainsail is slotted into a runner and hoisted up the mast.

Here, mention should be made of the different parts of the mainsail. The forward edge of the sail, just mentioned, is called the luff and the after or trailing edge is the leech. The lower edge of the sail is the foot and the corners are collectively known as the clew. Strictly, the clew is the lower aft corner of a triangular or fore-and-aft sail; the lower fore corner is the tack. This terminology also applies to the jib, which is the sail set between the bow and the mast, and to the spinnaker. The luff of the mainsail has darts stitched into it to give the cloth the necessary curvature when it fills with air. On the leech edge a series of pockets is sewn to accept short battens of wood or plastic which are used to extend the roach or curvature on this side of the sail.

The jib is hoisted by clipping it onto the fore-stay with a hank (metal ring) and running it up the stay from the bow to the mast using a halyard which extends from the foot of the mast to a sheave near the masthead and thence to the head of the jib. A sheet (rope or line) is attached to the clew of the jib by a shackle (metal link) or rope loop and runs to either side (port and starboard) of the boat, with complete freedom of movement through a pair of fittings. These fittings can be simple metal eyes, a pair of sheaves, a track and adjust-able slides, shackles or cleats.

An important means of adjusting the tension in the mainsail of a small sailboat is the kicking strap

Left:
A Soling surfs at high speed. Note the mainsail twist which is controlled by adjustment of the kicking strap/boom vang.

Aerodynamically clean spreader roots on this small section spar. The mainsail luff groove is riveted on externally.

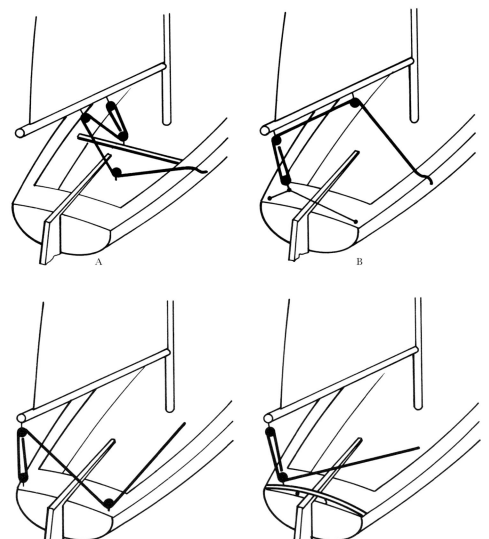

A

B

C

D

or American vang which runs from the boom, at a point some 18 inches from its fore end, down to a point just above the foot of the mast. When the mainsail is filled by the wind there will be a tendency for it to lift the boom. The kicking strap serves not only to keep the boom down but, to some extent, to bend the mast.

The effect of bending the mast is to pull the boom down and forward so that it bends slightly in the middle; the leech in the mainsail becomes taut; the masthead bends aft under that tension and the boom presses forward to make the lower part of the mast bend also. Tightening the leech by using the kicking strap has the effect of flattening the sail, which can be important when sailing between close hauled (almost into the wind) and reaching (with the wind crossing the boat).

If the wind is only moderate, tension on the kicking strap should be slightly relaxed when heading on a reach so that the sail is allowed to fill. In light winds, when a fuller sail area is required, tension on the kicking strap can be negligible or non-existent. Generally, the rule should be, the stronger the wind the greater the tension.

To the boom are also attached the fittings which enable it to be maneuvered at the will of the helmsman rather than swinging to the will of the wind. The sheet which controls the boom must obviously have a powerful purchase since it has to contend not only with the boom itself but with a mainsail which may be filled.

There are various methods of providing the necessary purchase using a combination of two,

A
Centered mainsheet. Here the forward lower block runs on a traveller providing control of boom angle and sail twist. The fall runs through a swivel block to the helmsman.

B
Aft mainsheet with center fall, more popular in the USA; the lower block runs along a rope or wire horse, the fall is led along the boom and comes naturally to the helmsman's hand.

C
Fixed aft mainsheet: a simpler system but control is poor.

D
Sliding aft mainsheet provides better control of sail twist. As with the center mainsheet, lines may be used to control the athwartship position of the lower block.

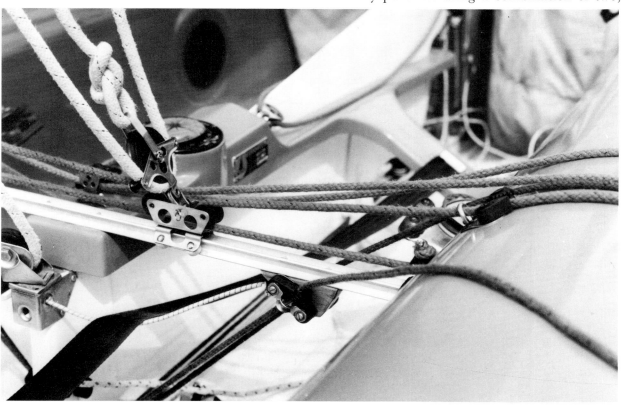

three or four blocks through which the sheet is run. The lower block, which must always be free to turn to meet the direction of pull, is usually attached to a horse, a metal bar fitted athwartships (from side to side). The horse can itself be fitted with a roller-bearing traveller which can be adjusted to port or starboard by ropes running from it to cleats on either side. On larger boats the traveller is a sliding one on which movement is controlled by adjustable lugs.

Within and around the cockpit of any sailing boat there is a considerable amount of other equipment and to the untutored eye that space in a small sailboat will appear to be bewilderingly cluttered. Even so, small boat sailing has been refined so much that the best sailor requires only essential and relatively simple fittings.

In the center of the boat immediately aft of the mast is the centerboard casing or housing, which is simply the protection for the centerboard that slides up and down inside it. The simplest centerboard is a flat plate which is literally dropped into the casing when the helmsman requires it to be down and is pulled out again when the need for it is past. A second simple type of centerboard is composed of plates which can be adjusted in the depth to which they are lowered by means of a chained peg inserted into the appropriate holes. These two types are known more generally as dagger plates. The more sophisticated, most efficient and least troublesome centerplate is pivoted and can be lowered slowly.

The principal purpose of the centerboard is to stop the boat making leeway. If a boat is drifting down wind, making leeway and the centerboard is lowered slowly right down, she will first turn and luff up, that is, swing her bows into the wind, and then slowly swing back to her original position while making less leeway. If a pivoted centerboard is lowered part way, the immediate reaction is different because the boat will fall away (turn away from the wind) but then, as the board is put right down she will tend to luff up. If a small boat is sailing in light weather with the wind aft the centerboard is really contributing nothing except a little extra drag. However, in fresher conditions it is better to leave it slightly lowered because it helps in controlling the boat if the wind shifts to any point other than aft. The centerboard also counteracts a tendency for the boat to yaw (swing from side to side) or dig its bows into the waves. If the centerboard is low the boat effectively has applied a 'brake' against making leeway and in some circumstances this can be a positive disadvantage. For example, should the boat start to broach – tend to swing around against the helm – a centerboard which is too low will prevent it moving sideways and the result, almost inevitably will be a capsize.

The point to remember about a centerboard is

The powerful mainsheet system here enables easy trimming of the mainsail. Notice also the kicking strap/boom vang lever system and the ultra-long tiller extension with non-slip hand grip.

that it develops lift in square proportion to speed. For this to become effective the boat must be moving forward and making slight leeway so that the centerboard has a positive angle of attack. Then if the sail side-force is increased by the wind, the boat's speed and leeway increase and the lifting force of the centerboard is proportionally increased to resist the side-force. If the boat is travelling fast the heeling component is relatively small compared with the thrust and the centerboard can be raised to, at the very least, halfway.

Continuing our examination of equipment in the cockpit, we come to the rudder in the center of the stern of the boat. This, when it is in the fore-and-aft position, behaves exactly like the centerboard in producing lift to counter leeway. This hydrodynamic effect is totally altered as soon as the rudder's angle is changed because, in effect, its new plane unbalances the various forces we have mentioned. As a result the boat alters its course as it seeks to re-establish the balance. The blade of the rudder behaves in the water much as a sail does in relation to the wind. That is to say, as the rudder's angle of incidence with the water is altered so the angle of force created by the water on the blade changes its effect, though remaining always at right angles to the blade. Because the rudder is held in position by the helmsman it cannot be pushed out of the way by the water flow; instead the whole boat is pushed sideways.

On some but not all of the smaller sailing boats, the depth of the rudder blade can be altered by means of a pivot and a line running along the tiller (the handle used to move the rudder) to a cleat near the pivot which joins the tiller to the

Opposite bottom:
A complex sailboat such as a 470 or 505 can seem a confusing tangle of string. Notice the lines to control the mainsheet traveller and the way control lines are led to the helmsman's hand. The compass, mounted here on the centerboard casing, is a useful tactical aid. Useful ideas are the shockcord to support the toestraps and the stainless steel guard over the self-bailer, which both protects it and ensures that stray ends of rope are not sucked through.

tiller extension. The purpose of the tiller extension is to act as an extra arm for the helmsman and give him or her the widest possible range of movement. It is, of course, invaluable in keeping control of the rudder when the helmsman is sitting out – a maneuver which will be discussed later.

There are various fittings for the toe straps which run from a point at the stern to the horse. Their purpose is to provide a point of purchase for the crew when sitting out.

One of the most important aids to good sailing is the boat's 'live ballast' – its crew, whose movements will play a vital role in balancing the various forces to which we have referred. The modern small sailboat is essentially a very light craft carrying, in proportion to its size, a large surface-area of sail. Inevitably this combination makes for an inherently unstable boat. It thus becomes extremely important that the crew should do everything possible to improve stability.

A normally well-tuned small sailboat will sail well even when heeling at up to 15 degrees but beyond that angle it is likely to lose efficiency and also to be in danger of capsize. The further a crew can sit out or hang out the greater the resistance to heeling. The positions adopted when sitting out can never be said to be comfortable but they can, at least, be made less uncomfortable if the straps are adjusted to suit the person using them.

A comparatively recent invention which takes 'sitting out' to its extremes is the trapeze, which enables the crew to be suspended completely outboard on a wire to make maximum use of the

righting couple – that is, the combination of the downward weight of the boat through the center of gravity and the upward hydrostatic pressure or buoyancy lift acting through the center of buoyancy.

There are various ways of fitting a trapeze but the description of just one will suffice to explain its purpose and performance. Essentially it consists of two parts: (1) a steel wire attached to the

Opposite top, left and above: The crew is ready to extend herself as the gust hits but once the maximum leverage is applied the boat is still overpressed. Initially the boat is in perfect balance but once the gust becomes too strong action to spill wind will have to be taken.

Opposite bottom: Solings starting a race in a light breeze. In such conditions crew weight is used to induce a beneficial angle of heel.

mast at the hounds (the point at which the shrouds and stays are attached), with a ring at the other end and a movable handle; (2) an adjustable harness with a quick-release clip or hook, attached firmly to the wire. The wire is kept under tension by a piece of shockcord attached through a fairlead on the side of the hull.

When the time comes to use the trapeze – which is when the boat will no longer be kept on an almost even keel by just sitting out – the crew slips the ring on the end of the wire into the hook on his belt or harness, using the hand nearest the bow to do so while his other hand keeps the jib taut. Now the crew removes his forward leg – the one towards the bow – from the toestrap and draws it under him so that his heel is under his behind and places his sole against the retaining fitting of the weather shroud. The fitting is usually a chain plate or a bottle screw and these will give his foot purchase. Taking hold of the handle on the wire with his forward hand he pushes outward with his forward leg, at the same time sliding his other hand along the jib sheet, then bringing his aftermost leg out to the gunwale (the rim around the hull). Once in this position he is able to release his hold on the handle and transfer the jib sheet to his forward hand. He is now completely outboard.

If the maneuver is carried out correctly the

handle on the trapeze wire is never used to support the weight of the crew through his forward arm; the body is supported by the harness attached to the wire.

To come back inboard, the crew takes hold of the handle with his forward hand, removes his aftermost foot from the gunwale and puts it on the side deck, bends his forward leg completely so that he can brings himself into a sitting position while still retaining his hold on the jib sheet.

As with sitting out, it is important that the crew should be suspended at right angles to the mast. If he is at more than 90 degrees his shoulders are likely to go into the water and he will have difficulty in getting back into the boat, with the possibility of straining himself and the equipment. The length of the wire is, therefore, of considerable importance and should be carefully worked out, remembering to take into account the fact that the crew's harness will stretch as his weight bears on the wire.

It will be seen from the foregoing that the use of the trapeze is quite complicated and requires experience not only on the part of the crew who has to do the actual work but also on the part of the helmsman in knowing when to use the trapeze, without overtiring the crew by doing so too much.

A feature of any boat with which we have not so far dealt is buoyancy. The ability of a boat to float is its natural buoyancy and this depends upon the successful balancing of the downward weight with the upward pressure of the water. If the downward weight is too great the boat will be low in the water and founder in heavy water, or even sink. If, on the other hand, the buoyant lift is too much the boat will ride high and be unstable.

It is the bottom of the boat – that part under the water – which provides the initial buoyancy, while the topsides are reserve buoyancy in that their floating capabilities come into play if that part of the boat goes under water.

Nowadays small sailboats are usually designed with built-in buoyancy in the form of air tanks which are part of the structure of the boat, or bags containing material with high flotation capabilities built into the 'skin' of the craft. Boats which have a great deal of built-in buoyancy will be found to be almost empty of water when they are righted after a capsize. In many respects this is obviously an advantage since the crew will not have to spend time frantically bailing. However, extensive buoyancy can also be a disadvantage for a less experienced crew since it means that after a capsize the boat floats high. The result is that the hull is more easily caught by the wind and blown along, possibly out of reach, and also the centerboard (which has to be used to right the boat) is difficult or even impossible to reach.

Good trapezing here – the crew is comfortably poised to come in or go out as the wind dictates and the boat is at an optimum angle of heel.

Opposite top:
The brothers Pagot sailing their Flying Dutchman in marginal trapezing conditions. The forward leg is bent and the foot placed on the gunwale ready to push the body out as a gust hits. The trapeze hooks onto a block running on a continuous loop with the trapeze wire which allows the crewman to tack without hooking and unhooking.

Opposite bottom:
Poor trapeze work on this Lazy E. Although the boat is heeling excessively, the crew's legs are bent and his feet are placed too widely apart, reducing his righting moment.

4 RIGGING

Dragons beating close-hauled in a choppy sea.

Having looked in the last chapter at the overall appearance of a boat and its contents, it is time to go on to examine in greater detail its rigging and how to get the best performance out of a boat by using the rigging correctly.

It is not at all unusual for people to think that the term 'rigging' refers only to the 'ropes' and wires of a boat. In fact it covers everything to do with the boat which is between the deck and the masthead – that is, the mast itself, the stays, the shrouds, the spars, the sheets and the sails themselves. The first three of these are known as the *standing rigging* in that to some extent they are fixed in position. The others are the *running rigging* which can be adjusted. Only by perfectly matching and setting up the two sets of rigging can a boat expect to be ideally trimmed and tuned.

On a sailing vessel of any size the mast is stayed from its top by stays (wires) which run fore and aft. The forestay counteracts movement of the mast to the aft and runs to the bow. Movement forward is countered either by a single backstay to the center of the stern or two running backstays to either side of the stern. This support is supplemented by shrouds which are wires running from the mast to the sides of the boat from one, two or three points on the mast. In addition to adding support, the shrouds help to prevent the mast from bending by easing the strain placed on it by the considerable tension of the stays. This arrangement is described as a masthead rig.

Usually a small sailboat's mast gains its support from a forestay running from a point about one-third down the length of the mast, and from shrouds running from the same point to the sides. There is no backstay. The shrouds are fastened to the hull slightly aft of the mast to counter the

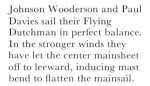

Johnson Wooderson and Paul Davies sail their Flying Dutchman in perfect balance. In the stronger winds they have let the center mainsheet off to leeward, inducing mast bend to flatten the mainsail.

forward pull of the forestay, which is attached to the stemhead fitting at the bow. The shrouds run to chain plates or shroud plates, which are metal fittings fixed securely to the side deck of the hull.

Raising or 'stepping' the mast is a relatively simple operation in a smaller sailboat. The foot of the mast is placed in the socket of the step which is either in a fixed position or can be moved a limited amount fore or aft in a mast gate. The mast is then pulled upright and held while the forestay is made fast to the stemhead and the shrouds to the chainplates. All are given just sufficient tension to hold the mast in place but no tighter because the angle or rake of the mast has yet to be adjusted.

A simple way of determining the angle at which the mast is leaning is to use the main halyard as a plumb line. The main halyard runs from the masthead to the foot and if left free to swing at this lower point, with some weight attached to it, will show the angle between the mast and the vertical. As a general rule the mast should be raked slightly aft. When the forestay is tensioned the head of the mast will be pulled forward. This is countered by shortening the shrouds to give the mast the necessary rake.

Determining the ideal rake is a matter of design recommendation, experience, preference, cut of the sails – and, in competition, of class rules which exactly define permitted rake. The degree of rake is not expressed either as an angle or as a precise

measurement because there are so many different mast heights. Instead it is expressed in millimeters per meter. Boats with flexible masts which will tend to bend forward would normally be expected to have a rake of around 40 thousandths. On a boat with a luff of six meters this would be 240 millimeters (ie, 40 x 6). However, the rake could be between 20 and 70 thousandths, which is where the variables of experience, preference and cut of sails come in.

Although we have mentioned putting tension on the forestay and shortening the shrouds, it is not advisable to apply so much tension that they are bowstring tight. Indeed, when the rigging is not carrying sails it should be relatively slack. Once the correct length of the shrouds has been determined to give the mast the desired rake, they should be fixed to the chain plates and allowed to go slack. It should always be remembered that the wires of the rigging will contract as the temperature drops; if they have been left taut during the day, their subsequent contraction as the temperature falls at night can overstrain the mast, even to the extent of giving it a permanent kink.

Having allowed the shrouds to go slack the mast will tend to sway but this can be prevented by bunching the shrouds together with a piece of shockcord so that they are putting some tension on the masthead. As they contract, the shockcord rather than the masthead will take the strain.

The requirements of a boom, which is attached to the mast at the gooseneck, are that it should be able to swing freely, that it is light because it is carried relatively high in the boat and, like any other spar, adds resistance, and that it should be flexible if it is to be used to flatten the mainsail by being bent. The boom is controlled by the main sheet or mainsail sheet, which must be strong enough to pull the boom in and out when the mainsail is set and filled and also to bend the mast when it is under considerable tension in a strong wind. The length of the sheet is decided by easing out the boom to its fullest extent – touching the shroud – and then adding that distance to the length required to run the sheet through the tackle system (mentioned in the previous chapter), through the traveller in the horse and thence to the securing cleat on the side decks. To that should be added about three feet (or about a meter) of spare.

Further control on the boom is provided by the kicking strap or American vang which, as has already been mentioned, stops the boom from lifting and also provides the means of tension by which the boom is bent to flatten the mainsail.

When tension is applied to the strap the boom is pulled forward and bent slightly down. This tightens the leech of the mainsail and also pulls the mast aft. The total effect is to tighten the

Outhaul and Cunningham are led by pulley system aft for easy control and facilitate fine adjustment of the mainsail.

Cunningham hole – pulling down the line flattens the sail and pulls the flow forward.

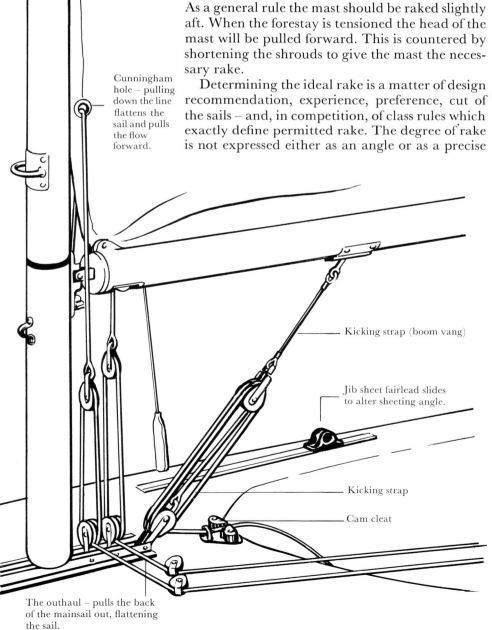

Kicking strap (boom vang)

Jib sheet fairlead slides to alter sheeting angle.

Kicking strap

Cam cleat

The outhaul – pulls the back of the mainsail out, flattening the sail.

Square sail and fore-and-aft sails

Staysails

Gaff rig

Working sails

Storm sails

Gunter rig

Mainsail

Spinnaker

Lugsail

mainsail so that it presents a smoother surface to the wind. In light or moderate winds, slackening the kicking strap or vang allows the sail to belly more, in effect forming a pocket to 'catch' the wind.

The extent to which a mast is allowed to bend fore or aft is regulated by the kicking strap while lateral bend, caused by the force of the wind on the sails from port or starboard, is controlled by the mast gate and by the positioning and number of spreaders used on the mast to adjust the tension of the shrouds to the best effect.

The spreaders are another part of the standing rigging and like the mast and boom, come under the general classification of spars. Again, because these are fitted high up, they must be light and should be shaped to present as little resistance as possible to the wind. Also known as crosstrees, they are pivoted on the mast but attached securely to the shrouds so that they do not slide up and down but are able to adopt the correct angle.

Before any sails are hoisted the boat should be positioned head to the wind so that the presentation of a 'wall' of resistance to the wind when they are raised does not cause a capsize.

Fitting the jib, or 'bending' the jib – as the act of securing any sail is described – involves, first, attaching the tack of the sail to the stemhead fitting at the bow. The tack of the jib can be

identified by the sailmaker's mark carried there and by the fact that it is the wider of the two corners on the luff of the jib. The sail is then attached to the forestay by the hanks, which are metal clip rings, working upwards from the tack and the halyard is shackled on at the head. The jib can now be hoisted.

The jib sheet is attached to the clew of the sheet either by splicing or knotting it in the clew cringle (the metal rimmed hole in this corner of the sail) or, if two or more jibs are likely to be used, by using a light shackle attached to the clew through which the sheet runs. The length of the sheet should be at least as long as the foot of the jib, from clew to tack, plus the distance from the tack to the fairlead through which it will run from the side deck to the hands of the helmsman or crew in the cockpit – then add about another 18 inches (or about half a meter). Though it is a matter of personal preference, the jib halyard is normally held in a cleat on the port side while the main halyard is made fast in a cleat on the starboard.

The first step in bending the mainsail is the same as that for the jib; find the tack of the sail. Again, the sailmaker's name is usually found on the tack and it is the corner formed by the meeting of the luff and the foot of the sail. At this corner will be found the bolt 'ropes,' which are the lines sewn on to the luff and the foot of the sail. The

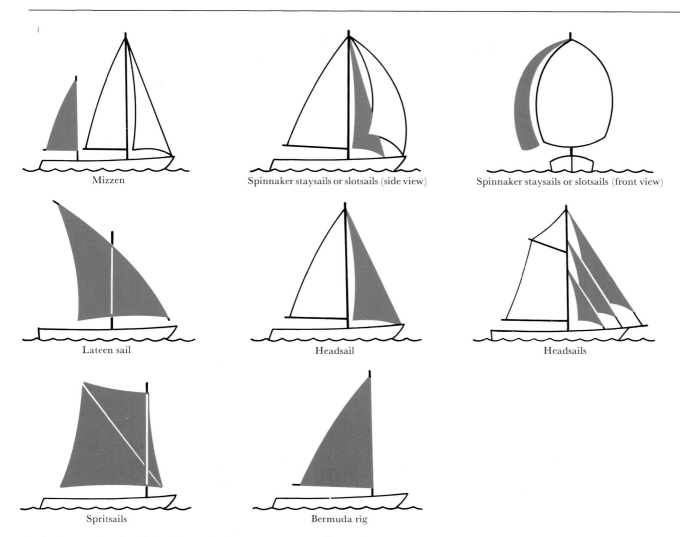

Mizzen

Spinnaker staysails or slotsails (side view)

Spinnaker staysails or slotsails (front view)

Lateen sail

Headsail

Headsails

Spritsails

Bermuda rig

bolt line at the foot is fed into the boom groove and made fast at the tack, usually by means of a pin, a hook or a shackle. The clew of the sail is made fast by the clew outhaul, with a lashing which should be passed through the cringle and then *twice* round the boom, making sure as it is done that the foot of the sail is taut from clew to tack.

The battens in the mainsail should be slightly shorter than the pockets into which they are inserted – except if the pockets have elastic tensioners – and should normally be tied in tight for sailing in more than a moderate wind but left under light tension otherwise. The battens should be bevelled at their edges and corners and kept well polished. They should be stiff at their after ends but flexible towards the forward ends so that they allow the sail to set to its natural shape. The main tension along the leech of the mainsail is in a line from the clew to the head but the area of the sail extends aft beyond this line. Without battens this part of the sail would flap in the wind, causing resistance to the smooth flow of the wind.

The mainsail is now ready for hoisting. The main halyard is attached by a shackle to the head board at the head of the sail. This is a rigid triangular section of the mainsail which takes considerable vertical strain from pressures on the sail and should be checked regularly for wear. There is some tendency when the mainsail is hoisted for the halyard and sail to pull away from the mast. In the majority of modern small sailboats the pulling away by the sail is countered by the fact that the bolt rope on the luff runs up the mast in a track. However, there may still be a pull up the leech to the head board and halyard. Strain from this can be greatly reduced by attaching a slug slide to the halyard itself so that it travels up the mast in the same groove as the mainsail luff. The sail is taken to the highest point it will travel unless there is a black band mark on the mast to show the maximum height it should be raised.

If the boom is attached to the mast by a gooseneck which can be adjusted in height, it should first be fastened in the highest position except in strong winds. When the sail has been hoisted to its maximum the boom is then pulled down until the luff is under fairly light tension. It is then made fast.

Obtaining the correct tension on a mainsail which is fitted to a non-adjustable boom is a different matter. In this case the tension has to be adjusted by using the halyard. It should be remembered that when sailing in light winds the sail will require its maximum bellying effect or fullness and that the *greater* the tension on the halyard the *less* is the fullness of the sail, since it will tend to be flattened. If the tension is too light on the luff the sail will develop horizontal creases near the mast; if tension is too great large vertical creases will appear.

Once the mainsail has been hoisted satisfactorily the kicking strap or vang can be tensioned and the lashing between the clew and boom should be checked for tightness, at the same time making any adjustments necessary in the tension along the foot of the sail.

There are a number of points to watch both before and during the work of bending on the mainsail. Each corner and edge of the sail should be checked for signs of wear. The tack is not subject to very considerable strains and so is not strongly reinforced. The clew, however, takes considerable stresses and will tend to tear between the clew cringle and the bolt line while the head of the sail will chafe between the luff line and the head board. If the gooseneck slides in a track on the mast, the screws holding the track to the mast should always be checked since they take considerable strain.

When the foot of the sail has been set up, check along the luff from tack to head to ensure that there are no twists. Before shackling the halyard to the head board, check that the halyard is not twisted or tangled and that it hangs straight from the masthead without passing round a spreader or a shroud. Make sure that the battens are inserted the right way round and are not rammed home sharply but are eased into the pockets. When hoisting the mainsail, do so smoothly, not in a

series of jerks. Always think about the way the mainsheet runs so that it is fed into its blocks to run in the correct direction without pulling against the axes of the blocks.

A further point to remember is that when preparing a small sailboat for the water you should avoid standing in the cockpit; the hull of a small sailboat is thin and without the support of water it can easily split.

Although a spinnaker sail would never be hoisted either on dry land – except when experimenting in the lightest of winds – or before casting off, it is appropriate to mention this type of sail here as it is part of the rigging. The spinnaker is a large balloon-shaped jib carried on the opposite side of the mainsail, set on its own halyard sheet and guy and with its own boom or spreader, which is used to spread the foot of the sail to present the widest surface area possible to the wind.

A spinnaker is normally set on a small boat

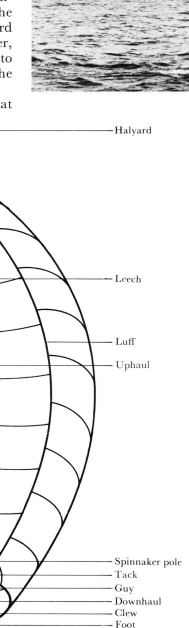

Halyard

Leech

Luff

Uphaul

Spinnaker pole
Tack
Guy
Downhaul
Clew
Foot
Sheet

when the craft is running before the wind or on a reach, with the wind coming from aft of a line drawn athwartship from the mast. Depending upon the size of the boat, it can be of a considerable area and should, at least, be equal to the total area presented by the mainsail and jib together.

The spinnaker, whether hoisted on a small or a large sailing boat, is the delight of photographers and artists since, with its bright colours and dramatically graceful shape, it is the most beautiful of all sails. To see any craft with a spinnaker running before the wind at full speed is a truly breathtaking sight – so long as the spinnaker is correctly set; if it is not, it will collapse like a burst balloon and sag in unsightly folds.

Although it may not appear so, the spinnaker, which is held at three points, has the same edges as a mainsail or jib: a leading edge (luff), trailing edge (leech) and a foot. The leech is on the starboard side with the clew at its bottom corner, the luff on the port side with the tack at the opposite corner. The spinnaker sheet runs from the clew to a block or fairlead well aft; the complementary 'sheet' which runs from the tack is called a guy and is also led to a block or fairlead. The spinnaker boom can be fitted to a fixed point on the forward face of the mast or, on slightly larger boats, in a track to allow for sliding adjustment. A wire known as a topping lift runs from higher up the mast to the boom to hold it at an upward angle to the mast and from the same point on the boom a line known as a downhaul runs to a cleat on the mast or near its foot to hold the boom down in fresh conditions. This arrangement is satisfactory for spinnakers of about 250 square feet (23 square meters) or less, which would be ample for small boats. Anything larger, up to 500 square feet (46 square meters), requires a bridle from the mast to the downhaul to lessen the chance of the pole

bending or breaking and for anything larger the topping lift and downhaul are bent onto the end of the pole, the downhaul running down to a fairlead or block in the bow and thence aft.

Hoisting a spinnaker in a small sailboat is a matter of considerable practice – to perfect the system which works best with a particular helmsman and crew, to save valuable time in a race and to ensure that the sail sets right as soon as it is hoisted. For this purpose, and also because of the sheer size of this sail, the rigging has to be set up on shore so that as soon as it is required the spinnaker has the halyard, sheet and guy snapped on. Each of these should run from the cockpit forward of the starboard shroud.

When not in use the spinnaker is normally stowed in the chute between the cockpit and the bow. It is folded in by pushing the middle of its foot into the chute and feeding it in until the tack and clew corners come together and drop into the chute. The luff and leech then follow so that the finished pile inside the chute has the head of the sail at the top.

Top left:
The retrieval line seen here from chute to spinnaker will pull the spinnaker into the chute as it is lowered.

Top right:
The spinnaker chute system is clearly displayed on this Shearwater Catamaran.

Once the boat behind has taken your wind there is very little your crew can do to prevent that spinnaker collapsing like a burst balloon. K77's spinnaker setting looks all wrong – the pole should be lowered and the sheet eased.

Since the spinnaker should set completely outside all other rigging, including the forestay, it is important to ensure that the halyard, sheet and guy should be correctly run so that they do not tangle or interfere with any other standing or running rigging. The halyard runs from the mast-head down beside the starboard shroud, passing under the jib sheet and in front of the shroud and thence to the head of the spinnaker, where it is attached by a bowline knot. The guy runs from the cockpit aft to its fairlead block and then forward under the jib sheet and in front of the port shroud round the front of the forestay to the tack. The sheet also runs from the cockpit to the fairlead under the jib sheet, round the front of the starboard shroud and then to the clew. The ends of both the sheet and the guy should be tied with a figure-of-eight knot to prevent them passing through the fairlead.

When the crew hoists the spinnaker he (or she) does so quickly, with the jib sheet behind him and the helmsman standing with the tiller between his legs to counterbalance the forward weight of the crew. The halyard should have a knot or stop slug

Flying Dutchmen prepare to hoist spinnakers at the start of a reach.

As the crew sets the spinnaker pole the helmsman is hoisting the sail – speed is of the essence in this maneuver when racing. Effective handling can win the race.

a few centimeters from the head so that the top of the spinnaker is not pulled into the sheave at the masthead. As he pulls on the halyard with one hand, the crew uses the other to guide the spinnaker out as it fills. Then he makes the halyard fast to the cleat on the mast as the helmsman pulls on the guy to allow the tack to come round the forestay and the whole of the sail's surface to present to the wind and fill. The crew pushes the spinnaker spreader out, first hooking on the downhaul and topping lift and then attaching to the mast fitting point. It is now up to the crew to control the spinnaker, cleating the guy and holding the sheet so that the spinnaker presents the best angle of 'attack.' The centerboard is adjusted to about a quarter down.

To lower the spinnaker it is advisable for the boat to be on a broad reach course, which is also the recommended course for hoisting. The sail should be lowered to windward. The crew must position him/herself near the mast with the windward jib sheet behind him/her. The spinnaker must then come under this sheet. Again, the helmsman stands with the tiller between his/her legs, holding the sheet and the guy. The crew brings in the spreader by unhooking its heel from the mast and detaching the topping lift and downhaul, and finally the pole from the tack.

Now the helmsman releases the guy and the crew hauls on the tack to bring the sail across to windward. The helmsman releases the sheet and the crew takes the halyard off the cleat and brings in the sail, taking the tack first and then working up the luff to the head so that the clew is the last to come in. The spinnaker can then be stowed in the chute as described before and the halyard, sheet and guy are cleated by the crew while the helmsman takes over the jib sheet and sets the boat back on course, lowering the centerboard as he/she does so. Once the stowing is done the crew takes over the jib.

Having broadly described the standing and running rigging, we should take a closer look at the great variety of fixtures and fittings which are involved in their use. The market for these items is today so lively and the introduction of new designs so frequent that it would be impossible to describe, even briefly, all the different types which are available. We can, however, describe the purpose of the most important fittings and the basic designs from which all refinements have followed.

As will have been gathered from earlier pages, a cleat is a fitting to which a rope can be attached. The basic cleat is a wood, metal or plastic fitting with two arms around which the rope is belayed (made fast) by winding it, usually in figure-of-eight fashion without using a knot. A *cam cleat*, now the most commonly used of all cleats, has two curved arms pivoted and sprung to open and close like jaws. When a rope is pulled through by hand the jaws open to allow free running. When the rope is left in the jaws the tension from the other end of the rope – from sail or spar for example – pulls the jaws closed to hold the rope in position. A jerk against the main tension releases the rope quickly from the cleat. When, as is often the case, the cam cleat cannot be positioned in line with the direction of the rope it is serving there can be a tendency for upward tension to pull the rope from the jaws. To overcome this problem cam cleats are available with a fairlead incorporated on the same backing plate and on the opening side of the jaws.

A *swivel cleat*, usually screwed to the floor, has a sheave and cam cleat incorporated in an arm which can swivel in a horizontal and a vertical plane. A *clam cleat* (not to be confused with the cam previously mentioned) has no moving parts and relies on grooved lips to grip on to a slightly 'kinked' rope. Ideally the cleat should be so positioned that the free end of the rope can drop down a little as it comes out of the cleat. A *tubular cleat* or a *trumpet cleat* is a metal tube through which the rope is run and jammed into a 'v' cut into one end of the tube. Its disadvantage is that it tends to chew the rope held under tension in the 'v' jaw.

Open cleats and *jam cleats* also have no moving parts but consist of one or two arms around which the rope can be wound, the jamming type having

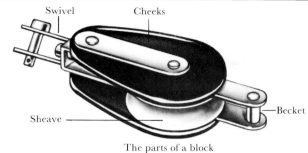

Swivel   Cheeks

Sheave   Becket

The parts of a block

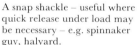

A snap shackle – useful where quick release under load may be necessary – e.g. spinnaker guy, halyard.

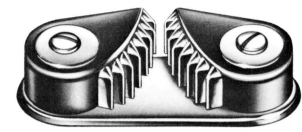

A cam cleat – the rope is pulled between the jaws of the cams – a quick upward pull releases the hold. Useful for sheets and control lines.

A Clam cleat – the diagonal teeth inside the groove grip the rope – a pull releases – for similar uses as the cam cleat it has the advantage of no moving parts.

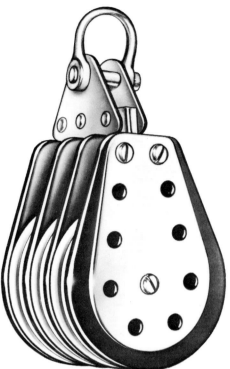

A triple block – used for mainsheet systems.

an under edge to the arm which increases in thickness from its tip to its joint with the base. The rope is jammed into the 'v' space so formed. There is an infinite variety of these two kinds of cleat, made in alloy and tough, lightweight plastic.

The center mainsheet traveller or horse is also subject to considerable variation, with a choice of types of track and of traveller depending on the size of boat involved. Some incorporate roller bearings while others rely on friction and manual adjustment; some incorporate cleats and fairleads on the carriage, others use platemounted sheaves on the carriage and have the cleats and fairleads on the side deck.

The kicking strap or vang is capable of considerable refinement to provide additional means of tensioning, the simplest of which is a kicking lever which incorporates a fixed drum, split down its radius. The wire of the strap from the boom is wound round the drum and through the radius. The other end of the lever incorporates a sheave to take the sheet of the strap from the mast. A small movement at this end of the lever is greatly magnified through the drum at the other.

Just above the tack of the mainsail is the Cunningham eye or Cunningham hole, through which a line can be passed round a sheave to a lacing hook or cleat on the boom to increase tension of the luff of the sail. The mainsail is fitted with strands of line known as reef pendants, which are used to make a reef in the sail by pulling down and roll-folding the complete length of its foot, thereby tensioning the whole sail and decreasing its surface area. The tack cringle is made fast round the boom, drawing it as close to the mast as possible, followed by the clew cringle at the other end of the foot. There is then a bunching of loose sail along its foot. The reef pendants are knotted to hold in this bunching. A relatively recent innovation, the reefing claw – horseshoe shaped to fit loosely round the boom and with rollers at each end of the 'shoe' – enables the bunching to be gathered down to the boom quickly and to be released easily.

Tension along the foot of the sail is usually controlled by an outhaul from the clew. The line is often made fast at the outer end of the boom and therefore cannot be easily adjusted while sailing. On high performance boats this problem is overcome, particularly on those with hollow metal booms, by running the line through a lead at the aft end of the boom, forward within the boom to a built-in block and tackle system and out of the boom to a cleat near the gooseneck. From that position it can be easily reached by the helmsman.

Control over the shape of the jibs can be exercised by extending the jib halyard from the foot of the mast up to a lever mounted higher up the mast. The halyard, fitted with an eye, is slipped over a hook on the lever. Movement of the lever, which is self-locking, is naturally transferred to the halyard to increase tension on the luff of the jib or to lessen the tension to give the sail a more concave curvature.

Successful control of tension on the edges of a spinnaker is also extremely important in gaining

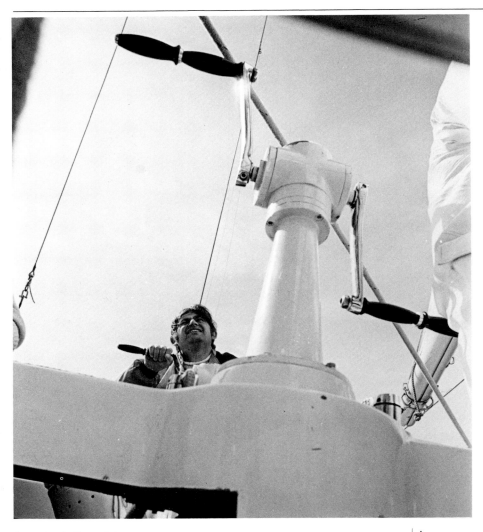

Large headsails need the power of these coffee grinder winches which allow the efficient application of two men's strength.

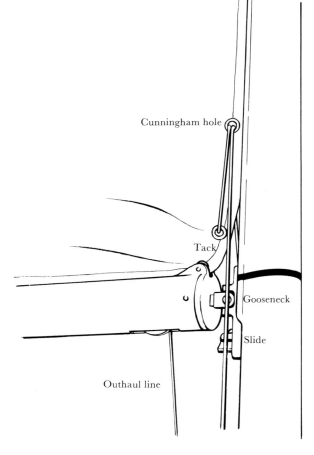

Cunningham hole

Tack

Gooseneck

Slide

Outhaul line

Use of the Cunningham eye adjustment enables fine adjustment of the mainsail luff tension.

maximum effect from use of this sail. The correct positioning of the sheet leads is essential, as is the ability to control the height of the outboard end of the spinnaker boom or pole, to which the tack of the sail is attached. One method of control on small spinnakers is to adjust the angle of the luff by using a series of knots along the halyard. These are used as stop knots in a cleat attached near the inboard end of the spinnaker pole. The top end of the halyard is attached to the mast by a shock-cord and the lower end by an eye to a shackle, so that the spinnaker lift and downhaul are one sheet. The outboard end of the pole can be fitted with a simple hook to attach to the tack or, for greater security, with a spring clip.

There is today quite a wide choice of masts available, both in terms of the material from which they are made and their shape. By far the most popular is the mast made from aluminum alloy, which has an excellent balance between strength, flexibility and weight. Masts of GRP (glass reinforced plastic), which first made their appearance in France, Holland and Sweden, are also in use but are expensive and do not show any particular advantage in terms of strength-flexibility-weight ratio.

Once the most common form of mast, the solid wood type, is now rarely seen except on older craft and small, relatively cheap sailboats. These are usually made from laminated spruce, to lessen warping, and have the metal track for the sail slides screwed on. The disadvantage of this type of wood, apart from all the fittings having to be externally mounted, is that it is heavy and presents considerable wind resistance, particularly in its nearly rectangular form. Box section wood masts present similar resistance problems, are also heavy and have the track fitted externally, though halyards can run inside to sheaves at the head. Hollow, oval-shaped wood masts made by lamination are an improvement in that the aft edge can incorporate a built-in groove for sail slides but this 'shoulder' adds weight and can disturb the pattern of airflow on to the sail.

Returning to metal masts, the least efficient are those which are made in two vertical halves, the aft extruded aluminum-alloy section being fitted to the forward section by a ribbed tongue on either side which disturbs airflow. The mast contains foamed polystyrene for buoyancy, can have halyards running internally and has a built-in groove for the sail. Far greater efficiency in terms of weight, flexibility, strength and least resistance is gained from the hollow, one-piece extruded aluminum-alloy mast. The clean oval shape presents very little resistance and the halyards can be contained in the aft section of the mast along-side the sail sliding groove. This type of mast can have the sheave cage riveted inside its head with a reinforced plastic sheave feeding the halyard down

the mast in the track position. The head of the mast is made watertight by a welded cap. The jib halyard can be taken through the mast by two sheaves, the forward one having a large diameter to reduce the bending strains on the halyard and the aft sheave smaller to enable it to be completely incorporated in the mast.

A stainless-steel gooseneck for the boom slides in the track of an alloy mast and can be clamped (or pegged) at the appropriate heights. The pin of the gooseneck is round at its aft end but square at the forward end nearest the pivot; when reefing is required the boom is pushed aft by the crew, rotated on the round section of the pin so that the mainsail is rolled on to the boom to the extent required and then returned forward so that the square section locks it in position.

On boats with centerboards, the rudders are always made so that they can be not only removed but also lifted when sailing in shallow waters. The blade will normally extend some 18 inches (46cm) below the water but will obviously create problems when in shallow water. Complete removal would leave the boat without a means of quick directional control, so the rudder is partly lifted. The rudder blade normally has two pivots (vertically one above the other) on its stock so that it can be moved in the horizontal plane. The blade is also pivoted in the stock so that it will move vertically

to alter its depth below the water line. A line runs from a cleat or hook on the tiller arm over a sheave in the head of the rudder stock and down to a pin on the blade. If the blade is metal it will drop to its full extent under its own weight and the line will be used to lift it; if it is a buoyant blade it will want to float and the line is then used to pull it down into the water. A sensible precaution is to attach the tiller end of the line to a length of shock-cord rather than directly to the cleat. If the rudder blade hits an obstruction, the shockcord, which stretches from the line to the cleat, will allow the blade to lift over the obstruction and then return to its previous position.

It should never be forgotten that the most important control of the jib is the sheet – when racing it requires constant trimming. In bigger boats this is aided by the use of powerful winches.

Right: Aluminum mast section. A single extrusion forms a continuous length.

Left: A wooden mast section. Two halves are glued together.

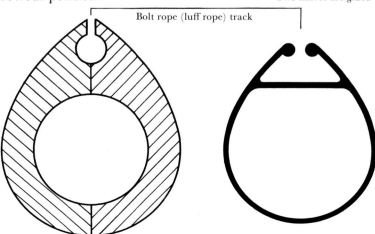

Bolt rope (luff rope) track

Rudder blades are now made of wood, metal or plastic. Wood has the disadvantage of swelling and shrinking, of distorting and of being more inclined to split – particularly along its grain – either from impact or age. Glassfiber blades can be more effective on all these counts so long as they are not – as many early blades in this material were – too flexible. It is important that the separate rudder head is really strong as it has to take strains from several directions and that the fittings or hangings are also able to stand up both to strain and corrosion. Rudder heads are frequently made of aluminum alloy with stainless-steel fixtures in all except the smallest of boats. Strength and ease of movement are also important in tiller extensions and these are best obtained with anodized alloy tubes which are fitted with stainless-steel universal joints allowing all-round movement. A useful piece of what might be regarded as gadgetry is the telescopic tiller extension which can be adjusted to suit individual helmsmen.

Any sloppiness in the movement of the rudder or tiller will reduce the effective performance and it is important to check regularly for signs of wear between the blade, the stock and the head, on the pivots, between the head and the tiller and between the tiller and the extension in the universal joint. Checks should also be made on the gudgeons attached to the transom to receive the pivots on the rudder head. As a general rule, screws should not be used on these parts as they are inclined to loosen or pull out under continual strain; rivets or bolts are recommended.

At least one anchor, anchor chain and/or line are essentials in every boat. The choice of anchor and complementary ground tackle depends first upon the size and weight of the boat – there is definitely no advantage to be gained from choosing lighter tackle than is required in the hope of saving money or effort in handling.

In a small boat stowing the anchor can prove something of a problem as there is really nowhere it can be put without getting in the way. It should always be well secured to prevent it from sliding and possibly puncturing a buoyancy tank or bag or from dropping out in a capsize.

There is a large number of shapes and weights of anchor, ranging from the Fisherman's anchor, traditionally associated with nautical pictures, to folding grapnel anchors (useful on board small boats for their relative compactness) and plow anchors which, as the name implies, look like a plow shear and are extremely efficient.

Though small sailboats require only one anchor, larger boats should always have at least two, including a kedge, which is a temporary anchor. On a small boat, anchor lines – not chains – should run through a fairlead at the stern and it is advisable to secure the line to the mast, using a slip hitch which can be quickly released if necessary. The line should be attached to the anchor by a fisherman's bend knot (see knots).

There are several advantages to using chain, including its resistance to chafe, its weight, which holds it on the bottom, and the shock-absorbing properties provided by the links. However, the weight can also be a disadvantage in that, when the chain is stowed forward the extra weight aboard can cause pitching. The size and length of the chain again depends upon the size and weight of the boat but two points are worth bearing in mind: it is not safe to rely on anything less than quarter-inch (6.3mm) and the length of the chain or line you need to let out is usually three times the depth of the water in which the boat is lying. Do not carry less than 15 fathoms of chain (90ft 27m).

The chain is joined to the anchor by shackles which should be one size bigger than the chain. The shackle pins should always be moused, that is, attached to the shackle by a flexible wire loop so that it is not lost if it drops out. The strong, pliable, locking wire is threaded through the eye of the pin, round the body of the shackle and twist-secured. In the chain locker, if there is one, rope – *not* wire or shackles – should be used to make the chain fast to the ring, using sufficient turns of rope to equal the breaking strain of the chain. There should be a sufficient length of rope on this lashing – four to six inches (10 to 15 cm) – to enable it to be easily cut in an emergency when it is necessary to slip anchor. When anchoring away from the shore an anchor buoy should be attached by a buoyrope to the crown of the anchor so that it floats on the surface above the point where the anchor is lying.

There is a multiplicity of fittings for shrouds and halyards made from metal and plastic for strength, lightness and durability: shroud and stay adjusters with series of holes through which the wires can be fed to give the correct tension; 'muscle boxes' which, through their hidden arrangements of blocks, increase the tension which can be placed on halyards while reducing the effort required; mast rams which adjust tension on the foot of the mast by the same means. These are just a few of the 'extras' which can be added to make sailing easier. They are, however, refinements which are best left until experience has been gained of the basics of sailing. The man or woman who learns to sail in a small sailboat which is fitted with every conceivable new aid or gadget is unlikely to be a better sailor than those who learn on a simple, probably less efficient, boat. If a boat is so equipped that it is virtually 'failsafe,' those who have learned to sail in it may well find themselves at a loss when they run into trouble in a less well-equipped craft.

The best sailor must have safety at the back of his mind at all times.

Reliable buoyancy aids should always be worn. For winter sailing a wet suit is essential for insulation and many clubs make them compulsory wear.

5 SAILING SAFE

One of the great attractions of sailing is that because it represents a challenge – man against water and men against each other in competitive sailing – it is also an adventure. It may, therefore, seem faint-hearted to mention the need to take full regard of all safety precautions not only while under sail but even before you leave the shore. Nevertheless, the greatest adventures were only accomplished successfully because those taking part exercised due prudence.

So far as the boat is concerned, the fundamentals of safety are in buoyancy, in watertightness, in stability and in ensuring that all the rigging is sound. Because a boat is large this does not automatically imply that it will withstand rough weather any better than a small boat, nor will a heavy boat be any more stable than a light one. Indeed, a light craft will often ride high seas better than a heavy one when it is hove to.

Whether sailing on inland waters, inshore, offshore or making passage across an ocean, safety so far as the whole crew is concerned comes down to a combination of things. Physical fitness obviously plays an important part and though it may seem obvious it cannot be over-stressed that a member of crew who is not properly fit can put the whole boat at risk, particularly if he or she attempts to conceal the fact. Part of the way to success in sailing is in building up a spirit of 'one-manship' as opposed to 'one-upmanship' in a crew, whether we are talking in terms of a helmsman with a single crew in a small boat or a skipper and large crew in a cruiser or yacht on a trans-oceanic voyage. Such a spirit will depend as much on mutual tolerance as on mutual respect.

Ideally on a small boat the helmsman and crew should be in perfect accord, even to the extent that each knows in advance how the other will react to a given situation. The person crewing must be prepared to carry out orders without questioning them. A good helmsman must learn to judge the capabilities of his or her crew and to be aware of signs of fatigue which will mean that the crew will not perform efficiently and may be in danger of suffering from exhaustion.

It is wise for a helmsman to remember the amount of physical effort involved in sitting out and to appreciate that an exhausted crew is not likely to be able to act quickly to maintain the stability of the boat. The crew has to move more often – and more quickly – than the helmsman. His main jobs are handling the jib, the spinnaker and the centerboard and maintaining stability. In addition he should deal with extra gear such as bailers, paddles, anchor, kicking straps and so on to ensure that they are secure and not likely to cause problems.

The weather, and the helmsman's ability to judge it, is an important factor in the safety of the boat and the people aboard. At first it is remark-

ably easy both to misjudge the weather when you are standing on shore and to fail to recognize signs of a change when you are on the water. For example, the wind never seems quite as strong as it really is when the sun is shining; and it is easy to stand in the lee of a clubhouse or a steep shore and believe that the wind is quite light, simply because you are protected. Even after you have pushed off and are still sheltered by shore or riverbank the wind may seem deceptively light but this may suddenly change dramatically when you leave the shelter and find that you are in a strong offshore wind – which is the sort of wind a beginner should avoid since it will make the job of returning to land very much more difficult. That is not to say that the wind must be onshore for a beginner as this will make return much simpler but departure will now be a problem! A gentle crosswind along the coastline or bank is ideal.

Before ever setting sail it is up to the helmsman to determine the wind direction away from the shore – simple enough if other boats are already out and not much more difficult if you study the waves or, on a river or lake, the behavior of ripples. It is also up to him to judge accurately the wind strength or to obtain this information from the coastguard or harbormaster, together with a forecast. Even if the intention is only to sail close in shore you should take the precaution of checking the forecast.

The opposite table of the Beaufort scale is an essential part of every sailor's equipment and the conditions which can be expected for each reading on the scale should be committed to memory.

From this scale it will be seen that Force 0 will be quite hopeless for a beginner to set forth in – or for anyone else for that matter. Even a Force 1 will be so light as to be of little assistance but Force 2, with the wind just marking the water with ripples and flapping the sails gently, will be ideal for a first sail, particularly if it is a steady blow rather than gusty.

The beginner who is sailing for the first time should never do so without supervision. If his boat is too small to take two people, an experienced sailor should be standing by on the bank or beach and the novice should ensure that he does not venture more than about 10 meters out. Later he can venture further out but even then he should always remember that even the most experienced sailor cannot always guarantee a safe return to shore if wind and tide turn against him. Every coastguard will tell you stories of having to rescue foolish sailors who have ventured too far from land and there is much to be said for French legislation which forbids small racing boats and racing keel boats from venturing more than two miles from a point on the coast where they can seek refuge, unless they are accompanied by a suitable escort.

Wind Force Symbols	Beaufort Reading	Description	Wind Speed (Knots)	Characteristics
◎	0	calm	less than 1	Limp sail, mirror-smooth sea
	1	light air	1-3	Small ripples. Leaves on trees rustle
	2	light breeze	4-6	Small wavelets with smooth crests, tree branches move
	3	gentle breeze	7-10	Large wavelets, crests starting to break
	4	moderate breeze	11-16	Small waves, a few white caps
	5	fresh breeze	17-21	Longer moderate waves; frequent white caps
	6	strong breeze	22-27	Large waves begin to form
	7	near gale	28-33	Sea heaps up; white foam; trees bend. Small boats head for harbor
	8	gale	34-40	Moderately high waves of great length; foam blown in marked streaks
	9	strong gale	41-47	High waves; dense foam streaks; crests roll over. Boats heave to
	10	storm	48-55	Very high waves with overhanging crests; surface largely foam covered. Visibility decreasing
	11	severe storm	56-63	Exceptionally high waves; sea completely foam covered
	12	hurricane	64-71	Air filled with spray, visibility seriously affected

13-17 are used for even more extreme conditions

The rules for all small-sailboat sailors should be: never sail on empty water unless you know that a means of rescue is close at hand; know the stretch of water you are sailing on and, if you are sailing off the shore, study a chart before setting out; be sure that you are capable of handling the boat in the prevailing wind and weather conditions; be sure that you sail well within the limits of the endurance of those on board.

The subject of safety also includes clothing. It is a foolish person who thinks that he can step aboard in only a swimsuit, sports jacket or ordinary 'shore clothes.' However warm the day may be, some form of protective clothing should be worn at all times. Remember two points: it is seldom as hot on board as it is onshore and the wind and sun can burn you more quickly when you are on the water. Remember, too, the dangers of cold do not come only from the water but also from the wind.

Heavy footwear such as classic sea boots are more of a hindrance than a help on a small boat and can be a positive danger in the water. Wear lightweight sailing shoes or gym shoes with non-slip soles.

Clothing should include underclothes, skin

suits, woollen and heavy cotton jerseys or light-weight but warm jackets of manmade fiber. The advantage of wool is that even when wet it remains warm next to the skin. One set of clothing is never enough, particularly if you are competing in a series of races – inevitably one set will get wet. Though a hat is not essential it is a worthwhile addition to the wardrobe; remember that one-third of your body heat can be lost through your head. In cold weather it can be advantageous to wear gloves but leather is best avoided as it can become slippery when wet, stiff when dry and will deteriorate quite quickly.

The effects of cold on the body cannot be stressed too much. In British waters and most of the eastern seaboard of the United States and Canada, the average water temperature is about 17°C in summer and 10°C in winter. In water which is 10° or less – and temperatures are lower on inland waters – the chances of survival through prolonged immersion are considerably decreased and at best a fit person may remain conscious for only about an hour. If the person struggles or attempts to swim, exhaustion, loss of consciousness and ulti-mately death will occur faster. That same fit person would have the chance of surviving fully

Opposite:
Crew of the highly successful German ocean racer *Saudade* is well protected against the elements. All are wearing lifeline harnesses.

Windsurfing is perhaps the most physically demanding sailing of all. In colder waters a wet suit is essential.

Children should always wear a buoyancy aid on the water.

Admiral's Cup boats *Rubin* of Germany and *Bumblebee* of Australia in the Solent. Note the plethora of safety gear round the stern including horseshoe and Dan buoys.

inflation tube protruding to within easy reach of the mouth. Alternatively the collar can be inflated by a gas bottle. The jacket, which contains some permanent buoyancy material, is fully inflated when the need arises and is attached securely by buckled straps about the body and under the crotch. On board the jacket is worn partially inflated.

While the life-jacket is excellent for keeping a person safely afloat it is not easy to inflate once the wearer is in the water but is restrictive of movement if worn inflated when on board. Greater freedom of movement is provided by a waistcoat incorporating individual buoyancy pockets. These contain buoyant material which nowadays is usually plastic foam. It is essential that the waistcoat is properly fastened at all times since, if left undone, it can easily force the wearer into a face down position in the water. This type of buoyancy aid, whether it is a slim waistcoat or one of the fuller kind which includes a collar, requires the wearer to be conscious and able to carry out minimal movements to stay afloat in a good, head-up position; it will not save an unconscious person. If sailing any appreciable distance away from the seashore is contemplated, and particularly if night sailing is also involved, the aid should also incorporate a whistle, attached to it by cord, to help searchers pinpoint the wearer's position, and a waterproof light.

Even though it is unlikely in the general run of small-boat sailing, that a member of the crew will suffer from hypothermia – the effects of extreme cold – it *is* possible, particularly if a boat sailing in blue water has got into trouble. It is, therefore, sensible to know what to do if you suspect that someone has become so cold as to be suffering from or on the brink of this life-sapping condition. Symptoms will include extreme lassitude, dryness of the skin, which will feel very cold, a sleepy look in the eyes (if the person is conscious) and a gray-blue tinge to the skin, particularly noticeable in the lips and often around the eyes. At one time it was recommended that the sufferer should be stripped and rubbed down and also given brandy or whiskey. In fact modern research has shown that this is quite the wrong treatment. Instead the person should be quickly insulated against the penetration of more cold. Ideally this is achieved by literally securing the patient from the neck down in a plastic bag but if one is not handy on the rescue vessel or wherever the rescue has taken place a sleeping bag or even a sail can be used. Failing all else, two or three people should huddle up against the person to shield him and conduct their own warmth to him. Thereafter the sufferer can be plied with very hot drinks so that heating is going on from the inside as well as the outside. A doctor should always be contacted at the earliest possible moment.

conscious for three hours floating in water of 17°C. The great advantage of a wet suit is that it is of very great assistance in the retention of body heat so that the wearer remains *actively* conscious for longer. The second stage of exhaustion comes when the person is unable to help himself or would-be rescuers even though he is still conscious. The third stage is loss of consciousness which is almost always followed by death.

An absolute essential for any small-boat sailor, whether a beginner or fully experienced, is a personal buoyancy aid of some kind. Designed to be worn by all members of a crew, they come in a variety of types. To be effective they should ensure that the wearer is not only kept afloat but that he floats face upwards with freedom to move. The best for purely floating purposes is a properly designed life-jacket with a minimum positive buoyancy of 35lb (16kg). It includes an inflatable ring collar as part of the jacket and this sits comfortably on chest and stomach, with an

Force 5-6 in the Solent.

At the risk of making this section depressingly pessimistic, it is necessary to consider what action must be taken if someone in the water is in danger of drowning. Obviously, he or she must be retrieved as rapidly as possible, the rescue boat being brought round to windward of him so that it makes leeway to him.

Remember that there are different types of drowning: one, which is least appreciated, is from shock caused for example by sudden immersion in cold water inducing cardiac arrest and rapid loss of consciousness; the other is asphyxiation brought on by exhaustion, when the person can no longer keep his head above water and therefore cannot breathe. Cardiac arrest naturally follows quickly.

Once the person has been retrieved from the water attempts to resuscitate him must begin immediately. If no pulse can be felt it will be necessary to carry out cardiac resuscitation at the same time as you attempt to restore breathing.

The recommended method for respiratory resuscitation is mouth-to-mouth. The patient must be stretched out on his back and his head put on one side so that any mucus, phlegm and water can drain out. If he or she is wearing dentures, these should be removed. Then tilt the head backwards by placing a hand on either side of the head and tipping it. This helps to extend the neck and open the respiratory tract. A life-jacket or bundled clothing can be put under the shoulders to support them and lift the head so that it inclines backwards more naturally.

Open the jaw and press your lips about the patient's mouth while closing his nostrils with finger and thumb. Breath into his mouth strongly: his chest should be seen to expand. Remove your mouth to allow air from his lungs to exhale and then repeat once every four or five seconds (12 to 15 inhalations every minute).

For cardiac arrest the treatment is to place the heel of one hand in the center (not to the left) of the lower part of the breastbone, extending your arm fully. Place the other hand on top of the first and lean forward to apply all your weight in two quick thrusts of pressure; return to full arms stretch and repeat. Ideally this should be continued at the rate of 50 to 60 thrusts a minute. However, if you are attempting mouth-to-mouth resuscitation at the same time and are alone it will be necessary to reduce the heart massage to five thrusts between each breath.

If the patient has clenched his jaw to such an extent that you cannot open it he is almost cer-

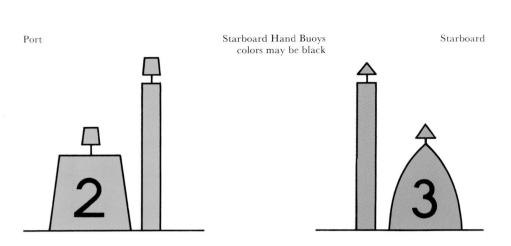

Port

Starboard Hand Buoys
colors may be black

Starboard

2

3

LATERAL

ISOLATED DANGER MARKS

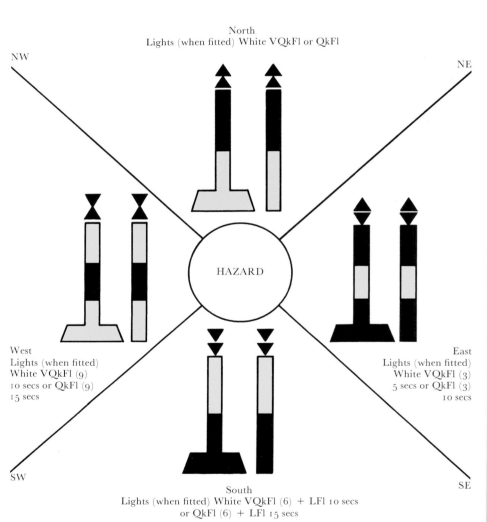

North
Lights (when fitted) White VQkFl or QkFl

NW

NE

HAZARD

West
Lights (when fitted)
White VQkFl (9)
10 secs or QkFl (9)
15 secs

East
Lights (when fitted)
White VQkFl (3)
5 secs or QkFl (3)
10 secs

SW

SE

South
Lights (when fitted) White VQkFl (6) + LFl 10 secs
or QkFl (6) + LFl 15 secs

CARDINAL

tainly in convulsion. Do not waste valuable time trying to prize open the jaw. Instead, breath through his nose, making sure that the pressure of your lips does not close his nostrils and also that you place a finger or thumb on his lips so that breath does not escape from his mouth as you blow

SPECIAL MARKS
Spoil ground, military exercise area, cable or pipe line,
recreation zone, traffic separation zone, Ocean Data
Acquisition Systems

SAFE WATER MARKS
Landfall, center-line or mid-channel

through his nose. Open his lips to allow exhalation between each breath. In the case of a small child your lips should cover mouth and nose and the rate of blowing in should be increased to once every three seconds. Cardiac massage should also be carried out more carefully on a child or elderly person because of the risk of fracturing a rib. For a baby the massage should be done using two or three fingers and for an elderly person use just one hand. As in the case of hypothermia, so too with drowning: the patient should be rushed to hospital as soon as possible, resuscitation attempts continuing all the time.

However, pausing only to emphasize that every sailor should be aware of resuscitation procedures and of the need to act without a moment's delay, let us now return to the water.

Safe sailing requires not only a knowledge of what is going on aboard your own boat but also what is happening all around you. What, for example, do all the various buoys in their different colors and shapes mean?

Prior to 1977 there was no established system of buoyage covering all countries in North European waters. However, since that year the IALA 'A' system has been progressively used. It combines the use of the Lateral system, organized on an international basis for ships coming in to port from the open sea, and the Cardinal system, once used only in French waters.

Lateral marks are usually either red or black. All red marks topped with a red can shape (red or white light), should be left to port when coming into harbor; all black marks with a conical top pointing skywards (green or white light) should be kept to starboard. The marks are numbered from seawards, red marks bearing even numbers and black marks, odd numbers. Obviously, on leaving port the system is reversed and black is kept to port, red to starboard.

The lateral system also incorporates marks to show the conveyance or divergence of channels.

These are black or red horizontal stripes or checkers on white. The topmark indicates the course to be followed.

The Cardinal system, devised to mark coastal and offshore dangers such as wrecks, rocks or sandbanks, is also simple and uses black and red as its basic colors. North is indicated by a topmark of two cones (triangles) one atop the other, pointing upwards and painted black. West is also painted black and has the top cone inverted so that the two 'balance' on their apex. South has the two triangles pointing down and painted red. East, also red, is shown by the cones base to base but separated by a gap. Each mark is placed in the compass quadrant to which it relates: a north quadrant would be placed north of the danger point; a south to the south of the point; an east mark would indicate a clear area from northeast to southeast; a west mark, a clear area from northwest to southwest.

Under the IALA 'A' system the combination of the lateral and Cardinal systems results in the following marks.

Lateral, used to define channels:

Port marks – red painted can buoys (round with a flat top) or spar buoy (showing only its mast above water) with a red can topmark; if a topmark is used, its light will be red.

Starboard marks – buoy painted green and either conical or spar shaped, possibly with a single green cone topmark pointing upwards. Its light will be green.

Cardinal, used to show the safe side on which to pass a danger, to draw attention to a change of course in a channel, a convergence or divergence. Buoys are usually a pillar but may be a spar, are black and yellow and always have black cone topmarks. Lights are always white and flashing:

North quadrant – yellow base, black pillar, very quick flashing or quick flashing (marked on

Opposite:
Incisif (Belgium) at the start
line off Cowes.

references as VQkFl or QkFl).

South – black base, yellow pillar, six very quick flashes followed by one long flash every ten seconds, or six quick plus one long every 15 seconds [VQkFl (6) + LFl every 10 seconds or QkFl (6) + LFl every 15 seconds].

East – Yellow and black base, black pillar, three very quick every five seconds or three quick every ten seconds [VQkFl (3) every 5 seconds or QkFl (3) every 10 seconds].

West – black and yellow base, yellow pillar, nine very quick every ten seconds or nine quick every 15 seconds [VQkFl (9) every 10 seconds or QkFl (9) every 15 seconds].

Other marks in the system include:

Isolated danger – pillar or spar painted black with one or more horizontal red bands, topmark of two black spheres, white light, two grouped flashes.

Safe water – spherical, pillar or spar painted red with white vertical stripes, spherical topmark, white isophase light (regular light and dark) or occulting (short dark, longer light) or one long flash every ten seconds.

Special marks – optional shape but unlike navigational marks, painted yellow, possibly with single yellow 'X' topmark, yellow light with a rhythm not conflicting with white navigation lights.

These marks should always be checked against charts to determine their purpose. Indeed, you should always check *all* marks against charts to ensure that you are aware beforehand of what you will encounter.

Though it is not directly a matter of safety it is as well to mention here the matter of successfully picking up a mooring buoy, which requires practice and good judgment of the way of the boat

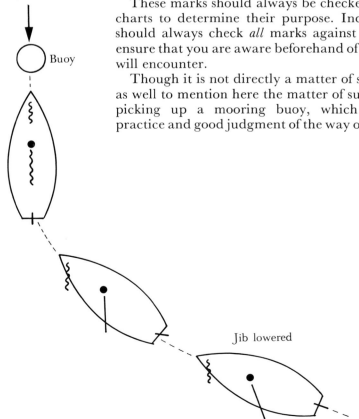

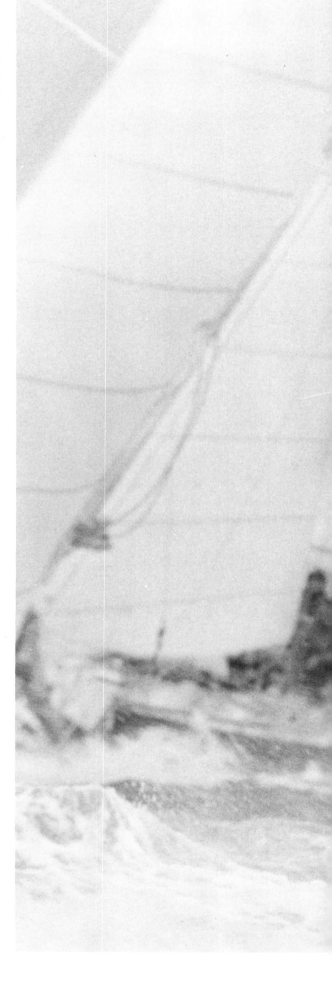

The scale of the problem! In practice, in open waters a big ship will usually give way to a sailing vessel as she should and it is improper to alter course until you have strong grounds to believe the other vessel will not. In confined waters, however, where a ship is constrained by her draft, a sailing yacht must give way.

and of prevailing winds and currents. Mooring gear is attached either to a mooring buoy, for which a chain rises directly from the bottom to the buoy to which it is shackled, or to a pick-up buoy, for which the chain lies on the bottom and light rope runs up to the buoy. For the small boat sailor the latter type has two possible advantages in that it is lighter to pick up from the water and, being usually made from plastic, takes knocks and even splits without sinking.

The best approach is made with the jib lowered if possible (and most small sailboats should sail happily enough without the jib) and the center-board raised. When you are about a boat's length from the buoy and approaching from a full and by position (down wind to port or starboard of the buoy) luff up by bringing the boat's head to the wind. This will slow the speed of approach yet give enough for the helmsman's actions with the rudder to be effective. (If the speed is too low the rudder will not 'bite' in the water.) Slacken the mainsheet right off while the crew uses the boat-hook to gather in the buoy rope. This is where the helmsman's judgment comes in: if he has luffed up too soon, misjudged the wind or current he will lose all the way before getting close enough for the crew to reach the buoy; if he approaches too fast he will overshoot so quickly that either the crew has no chance of picking up the buoy or, if he does hook it, is in danger of being shot into the water as the sailboat is pulled up too sharply and begins to swing wildly round the buoy.

Assuming the approach has been right – it will be, eventually – and the buoy has been picked up, whether by hand or boathook, the sails should be lowered and the boat made fast. In the case of a mooring buoy, a line is passed through the ring on top of the buoy and made fast to the bitts (the vertical members specially made for this purpose on larger boats) or to the mast. The line should be able to move freely through the ring of the buoy. Now the mooring is made more secure by shackling the anchor chain to the ring if the weather is fine or directly to the rising chain of the mooring buoy if it is rough. If a pick-up buoy is being used, simply bring it on board, following its line until you get to the bottom of the chain. This is made fast to the bitts by three or four turns – never attempt to knot it – and the turns are made fast by a line to the bitts or the mast. In the case of small sailboats the line will be the painter which is usually attached to the sternhead in the bow. If the weather is calm the pick-up buoy can be hung from the sternhead but in rough weather it is best to allow some distance – say, a yard-and-a-half to two yards (between one and two meters) – between boat and buoy.

Leaving a pick-up buoy or a mooring buoy can sometimes present difficulties though the latter is generally not as difficult as the former. With a

mooring buoy the chain is unshackled but the boat is kept lightly moored by a short line passed through the ring of the buoy. You will have chosen whether to leave your mooring on a port or starboard tack and the line is passed back through the ring of the mooring buoy and brought inboard on the side of the departing tack. Once the sails are hoisted and all is ready for departure the line is allowed to run through the ring as the boat falls away to its right course. With a small sailboat it is not necessary to use this line at all in good conditions; the boat is allowed to bear away by carrying the buoy to the right point towards the stern and then letting it go. In the case of a pick-up buoy a lot depends on the strength of the mooring line. If it is good the mooring chain can be unhitched from the mast and carried to the side while the boat turns on to its tack, the crew moving aft as the boat swings. However, it may be better in all but light winds to trim the sails first and let go the line when they are filling, without putting any strain on it.

Safety demands that you should also know how to guard against the risk of a collision. That, in turn, means that you must know the rules which are laid down. Depending upon the circumstances in which they occur, collisions can have very minor or disastrous consequences resulting

at least in hurt pride and at worst in damage and even loss of life.

Their avoidance depends very largely upon a high degree of alertness and commonsense as well as knowledge of the contents of *Rules for the Prevention of Collision at Sea*, which is available in concise form.

When under sail the rules state that you should keep out of the way of all boats you are overtaking; all boats on a starboard tack and under your lee (sheltered by you from the wind) when you are also on a starboard tack; all boats on a port tack and under your lee when you are on a port tack; and, when you are on a port tack, you should keep out of the way of all boats on a starboard tack.

Boats under power should keep clear of all sailing vessels; all vessels they overtake; all vessels showing cones, half-cones, spheres, hoisted baskets or lights one above the other on a mast; all other vessels under power on the starboard bow.

If you are sailing a small boat in a navigation channel and are approached by a large vessel under power, commonsense dictates that you take avoiding action. Similarly, despite all the rules, it is pointless to stick to your course – even if you think you are 'in the right' – if a collision will thereby become inevitable. The crew of the

Collision is always avoidable, always someone's fault; in the circumstances the helmsman of the right-of-way starboard tack boat looks remarkably restrained.

other boat may not have seen you or may be prevented by some emergency from changing course. At sea remember that nowadays large ships may well be on automatic pilot and unable to take prompt avoiding action; even with someone at the helm a giant oil tanker takes considerably more than a mile to change course. Inland, remember that many people who now take holidays afloat on powered boats unfortunately do not know or observe the rules.

The 'man overboard' situation is one which will not usually cause many problems to those sailing on inland waters so long as due account is taken of wind and current. At sea, however, it becomes a matter for instant decision and precise knowledge of the correct procedures. Remember that in all but the calmest sea the head of a man overboard will not remain in sight for very long and it is therefore important to get as precise a fix as possible on his position or the point at which he went over. In larger sailing boats the procedure is considerably more complicated than that for smaller boats but it is, nonetheless, well worth describing here as it contains several points which are of use to all sailors placed in the situation of looking for and retrieving a colleague in the water.

The essential in everything that follows the shout of 'man overboard' is complete coolheadedness on the part of all those involved. The helmsman must note the time the cry went up or the log reading and must remain at the helm since it is he who is responsible for keeping the boat absolutely on course until the other people on board are ready to start the search. Being ready means that all the crew have donned life-jackets and, on large boats, are harnessed. Only now can the helmsman bring the boat about. If the weather is fine and the sea calm the man overboard may well have been kept in sight in which case the boat can head straight back. But it is a very different matter if you are in a fairly heavy sea, running under spinnaker. The man may well be almost a mile or a kilometer away before the spinnaker can be handed and the boat turned back. Meanwhile a proper search procedure must be put in motion, a crewman plotting exactly how the search will be done. The turn having been made, the search pattern can either be a series of tacks with the wind ahead up a narrow 'passage' of not more than 100 yards or meters wide back to the position plotted as the overboard point, then widening to sweeps of about 200 yards or meters.

Masthead lights. A sailing vessel under 12 meters may combine side and stern lights in a lantern at or near the top of the mast. Larger yachts may in addition to their normal lights display red and green lights at or near the mast-head.

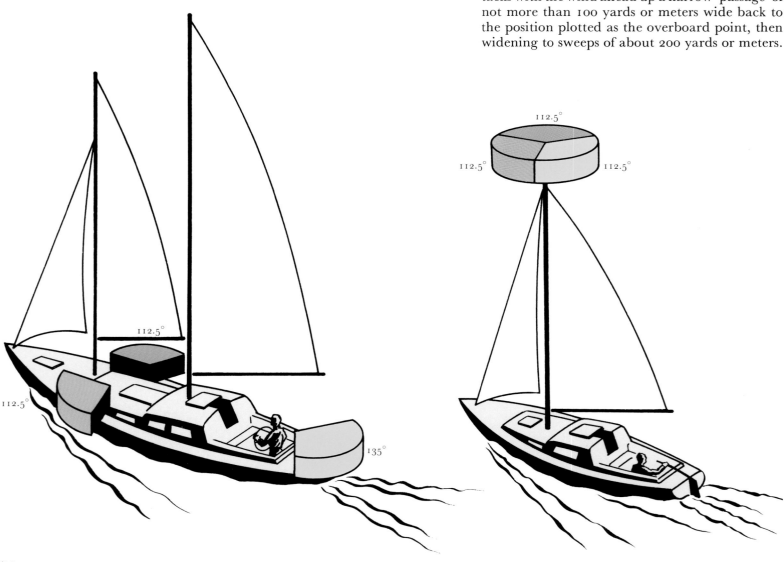

74

Alternatively, two wide tacks will take the boat straight back to the plotted point and the sweeps can start from there. Whichever pattern is chosen the crewman chosen to navigate the search must mark on the chart the time the incident occurred, the course, the position and the speed at the time. From that can be calculated the distance the boat has travelled from the 'overboard' call to its turn-back.

Picking up the man involves reducing speed to the minimum, heaving to on the windward side of him and drifting to him with the foresail backed and the helm down. If you fail to pick up on the first attempt bear away from him and complete a circle down wind and up to windward of him again to make another attempt at a pick up from the starboard side. With a smaller boat you can approach so that the man is on your port beam, tack rapidly and adjust leeway so that you can reach the man. In the case of anything more than a very small boat there can be problems in getting the man on board. This can involve at least one member jumping in, first having ensured that he is secured to a line, to help the victim. The boat has to be kept hove to, which may well mean dropping all sails and lashing the helm. And the man may be so exhausted that he has to be hoisted aboard by using the boom and the kicking strap or vang

as a pulley system, attaching a hook to his harness – assuming he is wearing one. If he is not it may be necessary to use the mainsail as a 'hammock.' The sail is released completely from the mast and is allowed to sink into the water before being brought up under the man, its clews attached to the hook and then hoisted.

From all that has been said about safety in this chapter it will be seen that it is a subject which ranges over practically every aspect of sailing. (The matter of capsizing, incidentally, will be dealt with later.) Regrettably it is a subject which some sailors tend to ignore yet to do so is to put themselves and others at risk. There is nothing unprofessional about observing *all* the safety rules *all* the time and the sailor who ignores them through a sense of bravado is demonstrating only that he is lacking in that most important of attributes for a *good* sailor: commonsense.

A muddy slipway is the start of many an adventure.

6 CAST OFF

An ideal single-handed boat for the beginner.

When you sail for the first time solo, whether it be with an experienced instructor aboard or with another beginner, the occasion is likely to be a nerve-racking one. The chances are that you will feel 'completely at sea' and will, for a time, doubt your own ability ever to be able to sort out the apparent jumble of lines and sheets. Small boats will probably feel dreadfully unstable and you may well want to hang on grimly.

Assuming that you have gone aboard of your own free will because you really do want to learn to sail, that feeling will pass remarkably quickly to be replaced by one of exhilaration as you discover that the boat does not turn turtle at the slightest puff or movement. The danger then is that you become overconfident and this is where the presence of an experienced instructor on board or on the nearby shore is valuable.

Ideally that first sail should be undertaken in calm – but not becalmed – conditions on smooth water with the lightest of winds. A fast-moving river, strong currents or moderate seas are all to be avoided, as are stretches of water which are crowded with other craft. Remember that you will not have anything on the boat indicating that you are a 'learner' and that, much as you may wish it at the time, there is no rule which says that other boats must keep out of your way. On a crowded stretch of water it may not be possible for them to give you a wide berth, even though the other helmsmen will quickly realize that you are a novice.

It may be that you would prefer to creep off to a deserted cove, hidden lake or empty river to venture forth for the first time. This, too, is definitely not recommended. You should be sure that you are not entirely alone; if your craft is solo there should be either someone of experience on shore or accompanying you in another boat; if you are with another beginner the same applies but if the other person in the two-man sailboat is experienced this should be precaution enough.

Remember the point made previously, that you should avoid setting out for the first time in an offshore wind and try, instead, to choose conditions in which the wind is blowing gently along the shoreline or bank from which you will cast off. Obviously, if you are river sailing and the channel is not very wide, this is not as important since you are not likely to come to much harm if you simply sail or drift to the opposite bank. Even so, it's a lot less trouble if you can be reasonably sure of returning to the bank from which you departed!

Let us assume – for your sake – that you have taken all the necessary precautions, are properly dressed and wearing a life-jacket or buoyancy aid, that the boat is rigged and you are ready for your first sail in a two-man boat, waiting anxiously on shore or bank. Hold fast, though; there may be

something you have forgotten. Do a check: mainsail, jib, tiller, rudder, centerboard, – yes; bailer, paddles? – no.

Always make sure that you have at least one bailer with you. If may simply be a small plastic bucket or it can be a sophisticated pump but whichever, it should be on board in the likely event of a capsize. So, too, should a pair of paddles which are invaluable in getting out of trouble of all kinds from becalming to the disaster of a broken mast. Ideally, they can be kept stowed away and secured by a line which will be long enough for them to be used without being untied and will prevent them floating off if you capsize or drop them. Make sure, though, that the line does not tangle with sheets and always make time to stow paddles and line away again after use.

The boat is on shore and there is a very light wind. If the boat is on a trailer and you are able to use a slipway it is a simple enough matter of wheeling the trailer into the water until the boat begins to float and then gently easing the trailer out from underneath. If you have neither trailer nor slipway, carry the boat into the water. Do not drag it since this will scratch the hull (causing increased drag in the water as well as unsightliness and unnecessary wear) and may damage or block the centerboard casing. It is important to ensure that the whole of the hull is floating and that the water is deep enough for it not to touch bottom when the helmsman and crew get aboard. If part of the hull is left out of the water or grinds as you step on it will take a terrific strain since it – and not the water – will be taking your full weight without any cushioning effect. Serious damage can result.

It is very much a question of personal choice as to whether the sail is hoisted before the sailboat is taken into the water or after. In calm weather it is probably simpler to hoist once she is afloat; in stronger winds or waves it may be better to part-hoist on land so long as the crew is capable of handling the boat into the water without it being upturned first.

The decision will already have been made about who is to take the helm and who will crew. Once the boat is in the water the helmsman holds her by the forestay, either standing in the water or on the jetty if there is one. As he does so the boat will swing into the wind, hence the need to hold her by the forestay since you want her to be bow into the wind, not stern first.

Now the crew climbs aboard or steps from the jetty, and hoists the mainsail fully, making the luff taut and securing the halyard on the starboard cleat. This is followed by the jib, which is also pulled up tight so that the forestay probably goes slightly slack. The jib halyard is made fast to the port cleat.

As he or she moves aft, the crew checks that all

Solings return to Weymouth harbor after a tiring race.

gear is stowed properly and that sheets and lines are not likely to become tangled. Having reached the stern, he drops the rudder into place in the raised position and fits on the tiller and its extension arm, checking that shackles are properly moused and that the rudder and tiller each move freely.

Now it is the helmsman's turn to climb aboard as the crew sits down on the forward seat or thwart. The helmsman lets go of the forestay and pushes off as he steps or climbs aboard and takes up his position at the tiller.

If the wind is very light and the boat is in a sheltered position it may be necessary to drift out with the current (on a river) or to paddle out to find the wind.

For two beginners this will be the moment when that sinking feeling is likely to be present and knuckles will show white as they both hang on for what they think is dear life. The answer is not to clutch at anything but to relax, to avoid panicky jerking movements and to help the boat maintain stability and an even balance by centering your combined weights as much as possible. The sails will flap idly and the boat will, indeed, not achieve true stability until they fill and all the forces we have previously discussed have a chance to come into play.

Since you have wisely chosen to sail in a light wind the sails will fill gently. As they do so, or even before if you can see or feel the wind coming, lower the rudder fully down. If you do not do so

the boat will probably just drift before the wind and, if the mainsail and jib sheets are not controlled, will turn so that she is side on to wind (beam on), with the sails blowing out at right angles. What you want the boat to do at the moment is to move forward with the wind blowing at right angles to it. This is called beam reaching.

Having lowered the rudder, the helmsman must sheet in the mainsail as the crew follows suit with the jib sheet so that they do not flap. The boat will stop drifting to leeward and start to move forward into the wind, so long as the helmsman keeps the rudder almost in the fore-and-aft position (helm amidships). The pulling round of the bow into the wind when the helmsman does no more than stop the tiller from moving to leeward is described as 'luffing up.' It is prevented by the helmsman pulling the tiller slightly towards him, so that the wind is on the beam.

With the wind in this direction and the sails sheeted, the boat picks up speed and both crew and helmsman will begin to feel the inherent stability of the combined forces. If the stretch of water allows it, this course should be maintained so that both people can settle to the feel of things. It is, too, a good opportunity for the helmsman to test the effects of moving the tiller to the left or right (port or starboard). The movement should be quite slight or he could find himself in all sorts of trouble.

At the same time, both crew and helmsman can take the opportunity to discover what positions they should take up. They will find that for this sort of course, they sail most efficiently with one sitting to windward and the other to leeward to keep the boat as upright as possible.

Small sailboats are designed so that they sail best in an upright position, heeling up to about ten degrees in any but the very lightest of breezes, in which case the heel should be deliberately increased to help the sails set better, reduce the area of wetted surface of the hull and give greater sensitivity to the helm.

Beginners will quickly find that it is an automatic, in fact an instinctive reaction to sit on the gunwale or sit out in the opposite direction to the heel of the boat. The heel will be to leeward and experience will show that as the boat comes back to an even keel they must adjust their positions so that it does not over-compensate and start to heel to windward.

The way in which the crew (meaning, in this context, *both* people aboard) position themselves to keep the boat to an even keel determines the *lateral trim* of the craft. As the strength of the wind increases, their efforts to maintain an upright position become more important – and more tiring – so that both will have to sit out, the helmsman using the tiller extension arm to steer a course and the crew making use of the trapeze (if one is

The crew weight of this Merlin Rocket is placed well forward so that the transom is lifted to the surface of the water. The crew is to leeward to induce a slight angle of heel and reduce wetted surface.

A Phantom on a beam reach – the helmsman is sitting well back to promote planing.

to the side of the boat from port or starboard. If the bow is pointing straight into the wind it is *head on* and the wind is *dead ahead*. At about 45° from dead ahead, port or starboard, the boat is sailing *close-hauled* with the sails sheeted hard in and setting flat. Falling further away from the wind means the boat is *full-and-by* and the sails, though still sheeted in, are filled by the wind. From this point the boat will be on one of four *reaches*: *close reach, beam reach, reach* and *broad reach* in turn, as the wind comes increasingly from the aft and the sheets are eased out. When the wind is from almost straight astern the boat is *running* and *dead before the wind* and the sheets are eased right out (see diagram).

Thus it can be seen that if we turn the boat closer to the wind than the beam reach which we are set on, she will be on a close reach, closer still will be full-and-by and a few points more brings her to close-hauled. To bring the boat from a beam reach to close-hauled requires the helmsman to bring the tiller back to the fore-and-aft center line. The wind will take her round through the close reaching and full-and-by position but as she comes through the close reach the sails will begin to flap because the boat is luffing (coming closer to the wind). The sails must therefore be sheeted in a little, just enough to stop them flapping and keep them steady across their wind-filled surface.

After an initial loss of speed as the turn is started, the boat will pick up considerably and 'come alive' the more she comes round in the full-and-by quarter. Beginners will notice, in particular, that the boat is tending to heel more and they will need to compensate by shifting their movable ballast – themselves – so that the crew is leaning out. They will also notice that the boat answers much more positively to the helm. Rather than planing, she will tend to be quite low in the water, which will probably be 'chuckling' under them, making the hull vibrate.

There is always a tendency at first to sheet in too much at this point, making the sails too hard. Instead, they should be eased and sheeted in again repeatedly: eased until they just begin to flap slightly and then tightened so that they are within a puff of flapping. Both by sight and touch the helmsman should detect that the sails seem to be trembling in tune with the vibration of the hull.

If you now bring the bow round a little more to the wind, the sails will again want to flap, but harder than before, and they should be sheeted hard in so that they are virtually flat. The boat will want to heel even more and the crew must work hard to keep her as upright as possible by sitting out but being ready to come in immediately any change in the wind brings the boat too far upright. There will be no more tremors in the sails, which will remain flat so long as the helmsman

fitted) to take him right outside the boat in the toughest conditions.

In addition to lateral trim, the *longitudinal trim* of the boat is important, though it is more likely to be overlooked. If the bow of the boat is too low in the water it is obviously not going to cut through the water as efficiently as if it is presenting as little wetted surface as possible. On the other hand, if the stern of the boat is overweighted it will tend to drag in the water, making the boat very difficult to steer and resulting in a drastic loss of speed.

As a general rule, the stronger the wind, the further aft the crew should move. The best guide is that there should be no undue turbulence at the transom. If the boat is sailing off the wind – that is, with the wind coming from a quarter behind – the crew should try to ensure that the transom is not immersed by not moving too far aft but if the wind suddenly drops both crew and helmsman should move forward to prevent the boat's stern settling or 'squatting.' The object is to get the boat to plane by balancing it longitudinally as well as laterally so that the hull is in minimal contact with the water.

Before going further with descriptions of the different maneuvers it would be as well to ensure that you know the different points of sailing – that is, the position of the boat in relation to the wind.

Mention has already been made of beam reaching, when the wind is at approximately 90°

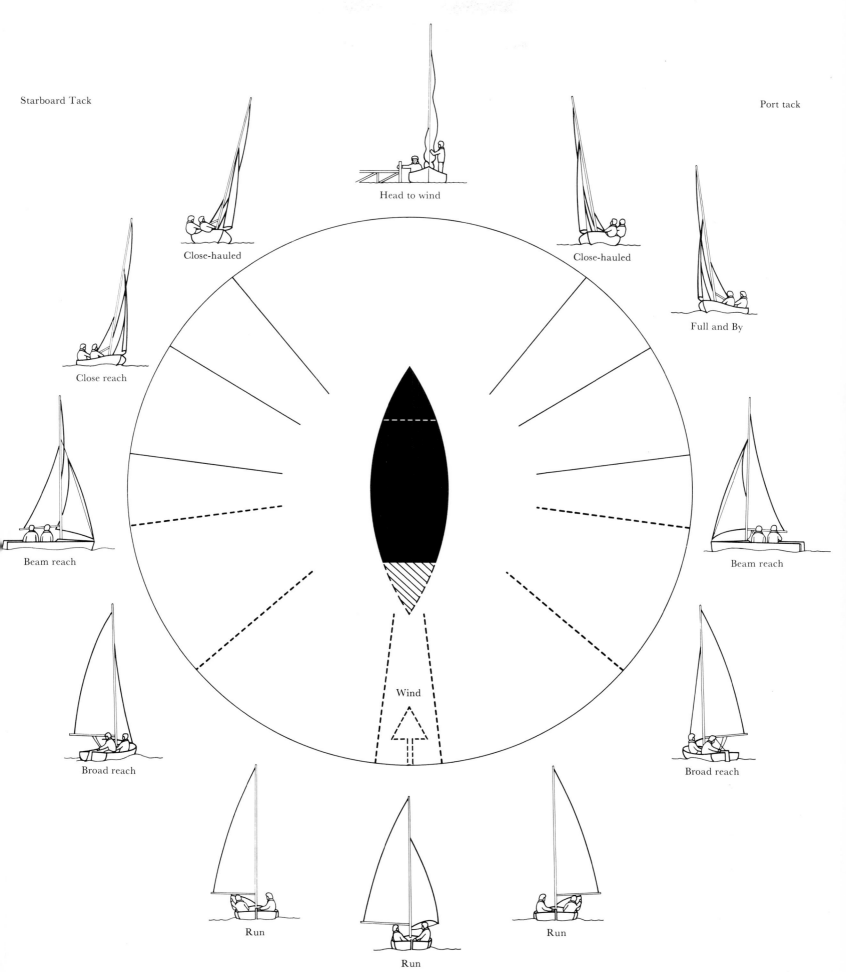

Starboard Tack

Port tack

Head to wind

Close-hauled

Close-hauled

Close reach

Full and By

Beam reach

Beam reach

Broad reach

Broad reach

Wind

Run

Run

Run

An OK sailing full and bye. The helmsman sits further forward to prevent the boat slamming into the waves and gains maximum leverage with the widest part of the boat.

maintains this course by keeping the tiller to windward. Now you are sailing close-hauled.

Maintaining the course at this point is not simply a matter of keeping the tiller in the same position and the sail sheeted hard in. In fact the boat sailing to windward will always be making leeway and must be pointed up to the wind frequently to bring her back on course. In effect what is happening is that the wind, though it is providing the 'driving force,' is pushing the bow away and this must be counteracted by the helmsman moving the tiller to windward against each push.

Inevitably the wind does not remain constant either in force or in direction and the helmsman and crew must be constantly alert to answer every change. If the wind increases speed in puffs, luff up a little in each puff so that the tendency to heel more is counteracted – with the help of more hanging out by the crew. At the same time it may be necessary to ease the sheets a little. Then, as the boat rights, bear away slightly and sheet in again. On the other hand, if the wind decreases the boat will heel less but it will be necessary to present a larger sail area by easing the sheets and

moving the tiller closer to the center line again.

It will be noticed that when sailing close-hauled with the sails sheeted hard in, the boat is not nearly as positive as she was when full-and-by, that she will tend to crab sideways and will not make the same speed. At sea she will tend to ride over the waves in a somewhat disconcerting, bobbing fashion rather than cut through them. If the sheets are eased slightly, she will become more positive, make less leeway and pick up only a little in speed. The answer is to bear away, bringing the bow further out of the wind by moving the tiller towards you.

Immediately the speed will increase and you can start again to luff up, ease out, luff up to find the right angle into the wind at which the boat achieves reasonable speed. If, instead of starting to luff up you continue to bear away the sailboat will still increase its speed through the water but only briefly. Then she will suddenly slow down dramatically and come upright. This is a stall, caused because the sail is no longer acting as an aerofoil but is presenting an obstacle to the wind, which becomes turbulent. At the same time the water around the hull will also be turbulent.

What has happened is that the angle of the sail to the wind has become so great that the wind or air can no longer achieve a laminar flow. Instead, the air is bouncing off and around the sail. The way out of this situation is to ease the sail right out, so that it flaps and bear away still farther. In doing so the turbulent pockets of air will be dispersed and the disturbed water left behind. As you sheet in again the boat will settle down and begin to pick up speed. This being so, you can start to point up again to come back once more to the close-hauled position.

Sailing close to the wind is by no means the easiest or the most efficient of courses and beginners inevitably find difficulty in achieving just the right balance which will give reasonable speed, minimal leeway and not too much heel.

Sailing a reaching course with the wind behind the beam is a very different matter and the boat will exhibit a different set of characteristics. Since we are leaving until later the maneuver of 'going about,' let us assume that we are back on that first beam reach. To bear away to a reach the helmsman must bring the tiller towards him (he is still sitting to windward) as the sheets are eased until the mainsail and jib are showing signs of starting to flap. If the sheets are not eased as the tiller is brought up, the helmsman will find that the boat is fighting to stay on a beam reach.

Easing the mainsail right out so that it bears on the lee shroud will bring the boat further round through the reach to a broad reach, when it will be travelling at high speed, heeling hardly at all and generally behaving well. All being well, this is probably the most comfortable and least

demanding of courses in sailing. There is no need for the centerboard, nor for the crew to lean out; the boat is making no leeway since the direction of the wind and boat are in accord; the hull 'sings' through the water, which seems smoother. However, the helmsman cannot afford to relax too much and must continue to be alert to the feel of the boat, which will react immediately and very positively to movements of the tiller.

For this reason it must be handled with care. If it is put too far to leeward the boat will be running dead before the wind, when the jib will fill if it is put on the opposite side to the mainsail so that you are 'goosewinging.'

Rodney Pattisson, Olympic Gold Medallist in the Flying Dutchman class, on a broad reach under spinnaker. The crew sits on the windward side to get the best control of the spinnaker while the helmsman steers from leeward to maintain balance.

A wind which is dead aft is one which makes the boat unpredictable – from being gentle when running on a broad reach it becomes temperamental and all too easy to mishandle. Maneuvers must be made with care and the tiller not moved suddenly, since this will bring the dangers of gybing unexpectedly or broaching-to. The latter involves the boat slewing round against the helm so that the sails are aback – that is, pressed against the mast with the possible result that it snaps.

If the tiller is put too far to windward there is the likelihood that the wind will get behind the mainsail and as the boat turns farther leeward the boom reacts violently by swinging right across, possibly cracking the crew painfully on the head and smacking hard up against the shroud. If the wind is fresh, damage to shroud – and head – can result and furthermore the boat will be out of control with all the relevant forces fighting each other rather than working in concert. The end result may well be a capsize – a situation with which we shall deal later.

To get the best out of sailing before the wind you should make sure that the mainsail is not allowed to twist so that the boat rolls about. To guard against this, the luff and foot of the sail are eased to give it a good belly, the kicking strap or vang being tightened to help resist twisting. The main sheet is let right out so that the boom rests against the shroud and the sail is at 90 degrees. However, if a spinnaker is available it should also be used, in which case the mainsail can be sheeted in a little so that the wind can flow easily off the spinnaker.

The spinnaker is hoisted as described in Chapter 4, with the spinnaker pole at right angles to the apparent wind and also to the mast. It should be allowed to open out as fully as possible while the tack and the clew are always kept at equal heights. This sail should be sheeted out as much as possible so that the foot is 'open' to allow the wind to flow out freely. If it is sheeted in too much the spinnaker

Single-handed boats are particularly difficult to handle down wind. The helmsman is trying to gybe but until he can restore the balance of the boat by easing the sheet, his efforts with the rudder will have little effect.

Top left:
The helmsman starts to haul on the halyard as the crew attaches the spinnaker pole to the mast. The spinnaker begins to emerge from its chute.

Top centre:
Once the halyard is cleated the crew pulls round the guy, filling the sail.

Top right:
Helmsman sits to leeward, crew to windward for optimum view of the sail.

Bottom:
In stronger winds, the speed of the chute system allows one to lower the spinnaker for the gybe and rehoist rapidly on the new leg.

will form a bowl which traps the wind. However, if it is eased too far the wind will simply fall straight out and the spinnaker will collapse. An indication that the sail has been eased far enough is that the top of the luff will start to fold back, in which case, sheet in a little. If the sheeting in is too hard a different sort of collapse will occur; the spinnaker will fold up in the middle and may wrap itself round the forestay.

Since the wind is not going to remain constant, use of the spinnaker involves repeated adjustments to ensure that it remains full. On larger boats these are helped by having the spinnaker boom in a sliding track on the mast but on small boats which do not have this refinement the boom can be allowed to rise slightly above the ideal right angle. Most of the adjustments, which are made to keep the wind well aft of the sail, are done through the sheet – that is, the line attached to the leeward corner of the spinnaker, the other being known as the guy.

When the wind puffs strongly the sheet must be eased as far as possible to spill the air. If the gusts are so strong and directionally inconstant that the boat is in danger of capsizing the spinnaker can be let go to fly freely out over the bow. This will naturally spill all the air and give the boat the chance to return to an even keel.

We shall return to other uses of this, the most picturesque of sails later but for the moment, keeping on the same point – sailing before the wind – prepare to lower the spinnaker.

For this maneuver the helmsman should stand with the tiller between his legs and should take from the crew both the spinnaker sheet and the guy. The crew then unships the spinnaker boom and unhitches the topping lift and downhaul before disconnecting it from the tack. Now the helmsman lets go of the spinnaker sheet and with the hand that had been holding it, takes the pole from the crew and stows it away inside the boat. The crew is then free to take the guy and gather in the foot of the spinnaker, working to windward. Ducking under the jib sheet he hands the spinnaker to the helmsman, then releases the halyard from its cleat and lowers the spinnaker. With the halyard still attached, he stows the spinnaker as described in Chapter 4, keeping the tack and clew separated. Finally the crew detaches the halyard and makes it fast and folds the remaining part of the spinnaker away so that its headboard is easily reached first when next it is hoisted.

Once the helmsman has handed the spinnaker to the crew he can lower the centerboard and trim

Top left:
Once a spinnaker blows round
the forestay, problems can
develop rapidly.

Top right:
The added power of the
spinnaker helps the Fireball
on to the plane in a moderate
wind.

Bottom:
Strong winds compound the
problems – speed and timing
with the pole are essential,
since until it can be attached
to the mast, the sail is
unstable.

Sweden's *Midnight Sun* thunders down the Solent in a typical August breeze.

Left:
An initial broach luffs K6087
sharply, wrapping her
spinnaker on the forestay.

Top left:
The helmsman's struggle with
the helm eventually returns
the boat to her proper course,
but the spinnaker sheet has
been let off too far; the sail
heels the boat to windward.

Top right:
Out of control, she gybes –
with her boom vanged to the
old leeward rail, she becomes
pinned down; meanwhile, the
heavier more stable 3181 sails
smoothly on.

the jib sheet so that this sail comes back into use again.

Changing direction from the point of running before the wind involves gybing intentionally, one of the most difficult of all sailing maneuvers and one which requires plenty of practice if the boat is not to gybe unintentionally – smacking the boom against the shroud as previously described – yaw (swing from side to side) or broach to (slew round and put her sails aback). The intentional gybe should only be carried out when the boat is on an even keel and running dead before the wind.

Before beginning the maneuver the kicking strap or vang should be tightened and the centerboard of a small boat should be raised by almost two-thirds because, if the move goes slightly wrong, it may act as an unwanted 'brake' in the water and cause a capsize.

Running clean before the wind and nicely upright, the helmsman sheets in the mainsail steadily, at the same time refusing to allow the boat to get away with its tendency to luff up by using the tiller as a countermeasure. The more the mainsail is sheeted in the less will be the tendency to luff up and the slower will be the speed of the boat. This does not matter: gybing can be successfully carried out with minimal speed. When the sail is sheeted hard in it will still be filled by wind from one side and a small change of course will be sufficient to bring the wind round to fill the other side of the sail.

As the sail fills, the helmsman lets the sheet run right out under control and also counters the renewed tendency of the boat to luff up on the new

tack. The gybe is completed, the mainsail has swung through 180 degrees and you can settle down and re-trim.

Going about involves changing from one tack to another when sailing close-hauled. Again it is important, at least for beginners, that the boat is sailing well trimmed before the maneuver is started and that it has sufficient speed.

Right:
This Laser is nicely balanced on a dead run.

The moment of gybe: as the boom comes over, the helmsman should counteract the momentum of the course change with a quick checking tiller movement.

Bottom:
The helmsman puts the helm down to tack; too great an angle of helm will stall the rudder and slow the boat.

As the boat is brought round through the 'dead' area, which is in the eye of the wind, the sails will slacken, begin to tremble and then shake as they lose all driving force. A small boat will lose its way very quickly because it is light and the sails are setting up a resistance; it should be allowed to pick up as much speed as possible before the maneuver starts. In addition, because it is inherently unstable, the smaller type of sailboat

must, of course, be maintained in trim.

If the helmsman bears away very slightly as the boat picks up speed but does not ease the sheets at all, he will feel the boat start to come about on its own. Now, if the mainsail is sheeted hard in and the tiller is released simultaneously, the boat will swing right about on its own axis. It will, of course, lose speed in doing so but being light it will recover quickly if the helmsman bears away and then comes back to the close-hauled position on the new tack.

If we consider the maneuver in 'slow motion' and with a larger boat in mind it can be seen that it begins with assistance from the mainsail. As this sail is sheeted hard in, the jib is kept as full as possible as it is tightened more gradually. Eventually the mainsail will lift and then the jib will empty and also lift. At this point the boat should have enough momentum to continue turning through the eye of the wind and on to the new tack. The mainsail will now fill again but you have to watch the behavior of the jib and delay trimming it.

If the jib is trimmed as soon as the clew moves over to the other side of the mast it will pick up wind on the wrong side, go aback and exert a terrific braking force so that the boat is brought up dead. Instead, sheeting in must wait until the whole of the sail is right across. Imagine a line joining its tack and clew: this must have passed through the eye of the wind before the sheeting in is carried out. The right moment has come when the shuddering of the jib has spread so that the clew is shaking close to the shrouds.

Movement of the tiller has to be carefully judged; it must not be too gentle as this will make the maneuver sloppy and slow, resulting in a loss of speed, nor must it be violent as this will make the rudder work as a brake in the water and jerk the boat about too suddenly, also resulting in loss of speed. Ideally, the tiller will virtually come about on its own on a larger boat as the mainsail is sheeted in, if the wind is quite light.

What of the crew in a small sailboat while all this is going on? It is up to both the helmsman and the crew to maintain the balance of the boat by shifting their positions uniformly as the turn is made. Both the helmsman and his crew will start off on the same side of the boat, sitting out on the gunwales or possibly with the crew leaning out. As the change in tack begins, the crew moves a little towards the middle but not yet to the very center as the boat will be heeling. As the turn takes her through the eye of the wind the crew ducks under the kicking strap and is right in the middle. Then, when the sail begins to fill again and the boat to heel on the opposite side, he steps over the centerboard case, facing aft, picks up the new jib sheet and goes across to the other gunwale.

Meanwhile the helmsman is working hard and

must transfer the main sheet and the tiller from one hand to the other, facing aft as he does so if the sheet is running from the transom but forward if it is through a center-mounted traveller. At one point, as the crew goes to the opposite gunwale, he and the helmsman will be on different sides of the boat until the helmsman does his change-hands move. This is all to the good as it helps to maintain the balance.

As with the tiller, so with the sheets: they should not be brought in violently but sheeted in gradually to avoid causing the boat to heel too far over. This is particularly important in strong winds since the boat will have lost a lot of speed and an extra strong puff of wind on an acute heel will cause a capsize.

Apart from the fact that a gybe involves chang-ing tack by bearing away from the wind and a tack or going about involves going 'through' the wind, there is another difference which will become most apparent if each maneuver is carried out correctly. A gybe is an abrupt change from one tack to another while going about involves the sail approaching the center line quite gradually and swinging over to the other tack smoothly; in an intentional gybe speed is maintained but in going about there is a loss of speed, though in a small sailboat it should be regained quickly so long as trim has been maintained.

It will be fairly obvious that going about becomes progressively more difficult as the strength of the wind increases and there can come a point at which the force of the wind and loss of speed becomes too much and the maneuver cannot be

Close-hauled on starboard. Helmsman pushes tiller away

Head to wind. Crew transfers weight

Resume sailing close-hauled on port tack

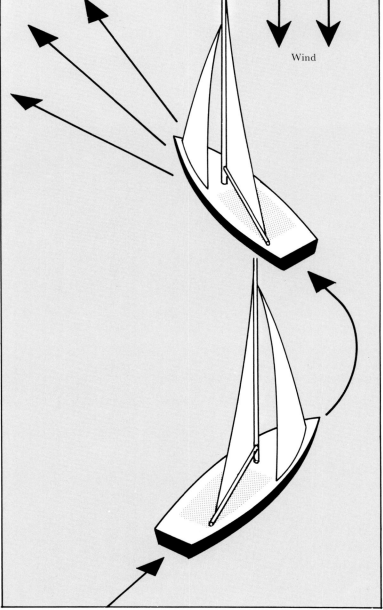

Wind

As this Cherub luffs the crew trims the sheets in.

mainsail to starboard and the tiller to starboard – this position helps to push the boat round to port. The boat will pivot to point well away from the wind. Now the boom must be released and the headsail allowed to fill tight. The boat will pick up speed as the wind comes on the beam and then, as the sails are sheeted in, return to the close-hauled position.

To begin with there appears to be an awful lot to do in a short time in coming about. However, it can be done without ever touching the jib because as soon as the boat has passed through the eye of the wind this sail will fill and force the bow onto the new tack, at which point the sheet can be fastened in the cleat on the leeward side. Admittedly, coming about in this manner means that the boat will lose almost all its speed and will only pick up if the helmsman bears away quite sharply.

A light sailboat will, as we have said, lose its speed in going about more quickly than a larger, heavier boat and this is particularly true in waves. It is, therefore, important to learn the knack, when sailing in blue water, of judging the rhythm of the waves and studying their pattern. There is, in fact, some truth in the saying that every seventh wave is a large one; usually waves come in series with a large one coming every fifth to ninth crest.

The trick is to start going about after the crest of the last large wave in a series has just passed. Begin the move either as the boat starts to come down from that wave or the next – smaller – wave, so that the bow passes through the eye of the wind as the boat is at or near the bottom of the trough. The next wave will, with luck and good judgment, come at the right moment to turn the boat as it is lifted.

An important point to remember is that, particularly in strong winds and rough water, you should try to allow yourself enough time to complete the maneuver without a panic rush and that you should never allow your pride to prevent you from breaking off the maneuver and starting again. That, of course, is more easily said than done if you are river sailing and the opposite bank is fast approaching!

If you fail to go about when you intended or decide against trying to complete the turn you may find that there is too little water left to leeward to try again. The answer is to gybe quickly.

Failure to go about from one tack to the other is described as 'missing stays' and the consequence is that she will be 'in irons' – that is, she will wallow about, turning neither to port nor starboard, with sails flapping and generally behaving like a sick duck. In these circumstances you must get the boat moving again by sheeting in the mainsail and the jib hard and bearing away. Then ease the sheets as you get moving, letting out further as speed picks up. Continue to bear away until you are running dead before the wind and sheet

completed. There are, however, various precautions which can be taken either to help when it looks as if the boat is getting into difficulties or to ensure that you go about successfully.

For example, if the boat appears as if it is not going to complete the turn because it has virtually stalled after going through the eye of the wind, the situation can be retrieved by using the jib. The trick is to hold the jib out on the side to which you are trying to tack. This will mean that you quite deliberately make it fill on the wrong side and go aback. At the same time push the mainsail out on the opposite side, making sure that the boom is held down to reduce the twisting effect. Simultaneously, reverse the tiller: if you are attempting to go on to a port tack put the tiller hard over to starboard. Thus you will have the jib to port, the

the mainsail as hard in as possible. The boom will come across and should immediately be allowed right out on the other side, followed by the jib. All this will bring you hard on the wind quickly but the speed of the turn can be checked somewhat by using the tiller to prevent the luff being too abrupt.

Returning again to the subject of the spinnaker: the act of gybing with the spinnaker fully set involves plenty of work on the part of the helmsman and crew but this is the only sail which can be allowed to remain full while the gybe is made. To ensure its fullness the wind must be kept dead aft all the time and the helmsman and crew must work together to maintain the best balance of the boat. To do this the helmsman must compensate for the weight of his crew being forward, doing so by standing aft at dead center with the tiller between his legs. This will help prevent too much fore-and-aft pitching but he must also help to stop the boat from rolling by transferring his weight as the crew moves about.

Either the helmsman or the crew first gybes the mainsail; if the crew does this he first hands the sheet and guy to the helmsman and then hauls the mainsail over, using both hands on the kicking strap or vang. Then the jib is sheeted to leeward

to keep it as much out of the way as possible in the maneuvers which follow.

The crew next moves to stand by the mast as the helmsman cleats the main sheet and prepares to control the spinnaker through its sheet and guy. Now the crew catches the spinnaker clew in one hand, unhooks the pole from the mast and clips it on to the clew. Thus, the pole is now attached to the clew and the tack, and the sail is now controlled by the sheet and guy in the helmsman's hands.

The crew works along the pole, hand over hand to the other end of it, that is – the tack end. He now unclips this end of the pole and attaches it to the mast before making his way back to his aft position, where he takes the sheet and guy from the helmsman, who has first trimmed the spinnaker.

A point to remember is that the centerplate is under the control of the helmsman during all the foregoing. The act of gybing will bring the aerodynamic force more to the side and leeway will be greater. To counteract this the centerplate should be lowered, possibly to its full depth. It may also be necessary for the crew to sit well out to maintain the boat in as upright a position as possible.

If the spinnaker is being used on a reach in

35470 starts to tack for 46391; in light weather a rhythmic rolling method will make for a smooth tack with no loss of speed.

Solings gybe at the wing mark. The foredeck hand of K116 is in the process of clipping the new guy to the pole. K106 has completed her gybe and is away on port as her rivals struggle to fill their sail.

anything but a mild breeze it will be necessary to put the crew even further out by using the trapeze to hold that upright position.

If the helmsman bears away too much it is very likely that the spinnaker will wrap itself round the forestay in what will look like a hopeless knot. Usually, however, the mess can be sorted out quite simply by gybing the mainsail over to the same side as the spinnaker pole until the spinnaker has untwirled itself. The main can then be gybed back to its correct side again, the helmsman this time ensuring not only that he does not bear away too much but also that he does not luff up. Almost inevitably a luff in these circumstances will result in a capsize – a subject we shall deal with a little later.

Returning to shore, river bank or jetty presents

its own problems and is not just a matter of driving up, putting on the brakes and switching off. If the wind is blowing favorably offshore the centerboard and rudder should be left down for as long as possible. This can only be done if the beach or bank is steep and you are sure of deep water until you are really close in. Remembering to raise the centerboard and rudder is by no means as automatic as it might seem and those who are used to setting sail from and returning to jetties are the most prone to forget when they are coming in to beach or bank.

If the landing is to be made on a beach it is sensible to look ahead to see how the waves are behaving; gently lapping waves will present no problems but if they are breaking to any extent landing will become more difficult since the waves

Throughout the whole operation helmsman and crew should bear in mind that the intention is to *touch* the boat onto land, not to bury the bows in it. Hence the need to lighten the load and also the essential precaution that the approach is not made by running straight in before the wind with sails goosewinged or spinnaker hoisted.

When the approach is made on a beam wind under good conditions the helmsman should luff up slightly. The centerboard and rudder are raised and the wind is allowed to nudge the boat into the shore. If the sea is rough the mainsail should be lowered when the boat is full-and-by – *not when the bow is into the wind* – and well to windward of the chosen landing point. It can then be brought in under the jib, with the helmsman ensuring that he keeps the boat at right angles to the waves. It may be that for some reason it is not possible to lower the mainsail when you want to; in these circumstances the helmsman must wait until virtually the last moment and then head up into the waves. The idea is to head for the shore with the wind on the beam and to raise the centerboard and rudder while still some distance out. Then luff up hard so that the boat comes almost to a halt as both the mainsail and jib are eased. The crew must jump out and hold the bow into the waves.

Landing head to the wind should not present any particular difficulty if the sea is moderate – and it is more likely to be when the wind is in this direction. It is best to choose the steepest part of bank or shore possible so that, again, the centerboard can be kept down until the last moment. The helmsman should aim to windward of the point at which he intends to land and approach by gradually bearing away, easing the sheets quite gently. With a reasonable speed up, he luffs at the last moment, the crew ensuring that as he does so the centerboard and the rudder are fully up. The boat is then allowed to drift in.

When the wind is directly aft and of anything more than light strength, the approach must be made without the mainsail, using the jib only. It is, in fact, possible to dispense even with the jib and to run in without any sails, 'under bare poles.'

will tend to lift the boat and propel it forward at an increased speed at virtually the last moment before touching. The bow will be pitched in and the stern lifted up and swung round so that the boat is beam on to the wind. The result can be an ignominious rolling about and scrambling which may give onlookers a laugh but is neither funny nor particularly good for the boat and the morale of those aboard.

Ideally the boat should barely be moving as she approaches the shore and the crew should step into the water at the earliest opportunity to lighten her and keep her stern to the waves. (In fact, in a freeing wind it is best – indeed, necessary – to make the approach stern-first so that the bows are taking the waves but this requires a 180-degree turn and needs plenty of practice.)

Mooring alongside a pontoon or quay.

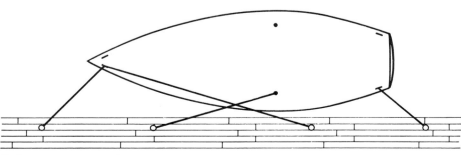

Spring ropes prevent surging.

Practice in gentle winds can seem easy but righting a boat in strong winds, particularly a heavy single-hander, can demand strength and endurance.

7 CAPSIZING AND AFTER

Once upright again start sailing as quickly as possible to clear the boat of water through her self-bailers.

One experienced yachtsman once told me that every sailor should deliberately capsize his boat once to find out what it was like and how to cope with the situation. Thereafter any capsize could be considered a mistake since no one but a fool would do so deliberately more than once!

To watchers from the safety of the shore a capsize is usually regarded as a welcome diversion and a bit of excitement; to fellow sailors it may be a cause for amusement or, if it happens in a race, for satisfaction. To those who are actually involved, however, it is not merely an annoyance it is a possible danger, can result in damage and injury or worse and is something which, since it has not been avoided, must be put right as quickly as possible, *without panic*.

Almost without exception the capsize will occur

to leeward when the boat heels too far over and, with the sails hard in, has not enough speed to recover its equilibrium. It may happen suddenly, with virtually no warning or slowly, the boat gradually heeling farther and farther over in what seems and feels like an agonizing slow motion replay.

If the capsize is sudden there is very little that those on board can do, but when the situation

comes about gradually there is no point in just sitting there waiting for the apparently inevitable ducking. By letting go of the sheets and of the helm the boat *may* come up into the wind and right itself.

The sensible sailor will always bear in mind the possibility of a capsize, no matter how experienced he may be. To this end, he will always try to ensure that everything is kept in order on board, that sheets are correctly fastened without long trailing ends, that lines are coiled, poles and paddles stowed and fastened by shockcord, spare sails kept in their bags or, in the case of the spinnaker with a chute, properly folded away. Anything that is detachable and likely to come free and float off or sink in a capsize should be lashed, moused or corded so that it remains with the upturned hull in the event of a capsize.

Halyards which are not tensioned through levers but are attached directly to cleats should always be fastened in such a way that they can be released quickly because it may be necessary to get the sails down in as short a time as possible.

The most important thing in a capsize is to try to prevent the boat from turning completely upside down so that the mast is pointing straight down in the water. In these circumstances there is always the real danger that the mast will stick into mud or sand or foul rocks and may be bent or broken. The job of righting the boat from the mast-down position becomes almost impossible without extra assistance.

Let us assume, however, that the capsize is a straightforward tipping over to leeward and the boat is lying on its side. One of the two people on board – usually the crewman – must jump or slide into the water to leeward and hold on to the bow to try to keep it pointing into the wind. Whatever happens neither the crew nor the helmsman must attempt to hang on to anything inside the boat; that includes halyards, shrouds, sheets, tiller or tiller extension, shockcords and so on. Nor, under any circumstances, must the helmsman or crew attempt to gain support by standing on anything inside the boat such as the mast, boom or centerplate case. Apart from the possibility of causing damage, the act of standing on any of these will turn the boat further under and increase the likelihood of it turning turtle completely.

As the crew in the water works his way to the bow the helmsman gets the sails down and then, keeping his weight well aft, climbs over the gunwale and stands on the centerboard. This is the only point on which leverage can be applied to lift the boat upright. If the centerboard was not down when the capsize occurred it has to be extended now. This will mean that the crew has to leave the bow and go round the hull to pull at the board while the helmsman pushes at it from the other side.

The catamaran *Nacra*, a Dutch entry sailed by Schuitema in the John Player World Speed Trials at Weymouth, takes a nosedive during high winds. The boat was undamaged and continued to sail, eventually clocking the fastest speed of the day.

With both the crew of this Hornet on the centerboard she will come up easily enough, but with the main and spinnaker still hoisted further problems could follow.

If both the crew and the helmsman have been thrown into the water by the capsize they must swim round to the centerboard. All being well — or as well as things can be in these circumstances — the centerboard will be lying on the surface of the water or sticking out slightly above it. Fate, however, frequently decrees that this is not the case and the board is found to be at an angle well out of the water. If one of the crew has managed to stay on board this is no great problem as he will be able to climb over the gunwale and stand on the centerboard relatively easily. But if both men are in the water, reaching up for the centerboard can be both difficult and tiring. It may be possible for both to extend their arms fully and get a grip on the centerboard to drag it down. On the other hand reaching it may involve one man 'bouncing' himself in the water and trying to jump up for the board while the other gives him what leverage he can. No easy matter when wearing a life-jacket or buoyancy aid and wet clothes.

Once the centerboard has been brought down to water level and pushed under, one man should go back to the bow and try to bring it back to point into the wind, while the other climbs on to it and grasps the gunwale. Then he leans back to

exert full leverage. Usually the boat will come upright.

If the boat has turned over completely, one of the crew must climb up on to the hull and lever his weight against the protruding centerboard to bring it down to the water. Then he stands on the board and carries on as we have already described.

The chances are that when the boat has been righted it will contain a lot of water. Though boats with extensive built-in buoyancy will often be virtually empty they are much more difficult to right because they ride high out of the water and the centerboard is that much more difficult to

reach. In addition they present a greater surface area to the wind and are therefore carried down-wind more rapidly than a lower lying boat. A boat full of water is extremely unstable and will tip over again given the slightest chance. On no account should both members of the crew try to get in over the side. One man goes in over the transom while the other remains in the water, holding on to the side. The man on board immediately starts to bail. We are assuming that the precaution of securing the bailer has been taken but if it has not, it is possible to bail fairly successfully with a shirt, trousers, nylon jacket or with a sailbag if an empty

As she comes up, the boat rounds up into the wind; the quicker the crew can get aboard, the more chance they have of controlling things.

one is not in use and readily accessible.

When the boat is riding more out of the water and has taken on a greater degree of stability the man in the water can come aboard, being helped in over the transom. Both then continue bailing and making things generally shipshape.

There are numerous important points to remember regarding the events which occur in a capsize. For example, the boat will lie across the wind and will drift before the wind, travelling hull first. If you attempt to right the boat with the mast pointing into the wind and the sails still up, there is a strong possibility that the boat will come upright and immediately tip over the other way (to leeward), coming down on top of you. The weight of a water-filled hull plus mast and sodden sails is considerable and injury is quite possible in these circumstances.

If the wind is strong – which, of course is when most capsizes occur – the boat should be turned until its mast points downwind. It is then levered up against the wind. Though extra effort is required it is worthwhile.

A useful tip is to keep the boat's anchor in such a position that if the capsize involves a complete turnover it will be able to fall freely to the bottom and hold the boat against the wind and current.

Though it is very often not done, it is a good idea for the man who is standing on the centerboard to catch hold of the jib sheet, if he can. He can then pull it through the fairlead until the restraining knot stops it. Now he can lean back on the sheet, using its length to gain extra leverage.

A capsize when sailing under spinnaker (which probably means that the wind was too strong for the spinnaker to have been in use in the first place), will involve a considerable amount of sorting out of tangled ropes and sails *before* attempting to right the boat. One man should do this while the other holds the boat in a horizontal position by sitting or standing on the centerboard without putting on any leverage.

A small sailboat that holds a great deal of water becomes extremely difficult to right and if the crew are inexperienced or not particularly fit they should decide quickly, after a few attempts at righting, whether to continue their efforts alone or wait for help.

The act of righting a capsized boat is usually very tiring unless you are extremely lucky and can bring it upright virtually in two moves – over the gunwale to the centerboard and heave – while the sails are lying on the surface of the water. Though we have recommended carrying out deliberate capsizes to gain practice, beginners will become exhausted if they are called upon to carry out more than a couple of capsizes at once. Even experienced sailors should think twice about the number of times they attempt to right a boat should they be unfortunate enough to capsize

The dreaded capsize to windward on a run with the boom too far out, this OK rolls to windward.

Failure to haul in the mainsheet to counteract results in capsize.

Righting commences but with the mast to windward!

A further capsize on top of the helmsman is practically inevitable.

several times running. (If they do, incidentally, though experienced, they are not good sailors!) There will come a point when exhaustion will set in and, assuming that other craft are about, it may be better to wait for assistance and pride be damned!

A boat which has a metal mast will have a greater tendency to turn mast-down, particularly if it is hollow. The tubular mast will fill rapidly with water and drag the boat further round until it has completed a 180 degree inversion. Thereafter, the weight of water inside the mast will make for even greater difficulty in righting the boat and may well defeat all efforts. Ideally, the hollow metal mast should be filled with non-absorbent lightweight foam.

If the mast is left hollow and the crew actually succeed in righting the boat there is a very real possibility that the weight of water will make the craft so top-heavy that it tips over the other way. If it does not and the boat remains in a precarious upright position, do not spoil things by trying to climb aboard straight away. Give the water in the mast time to drain out first.

Under no circumstances should you leave a capsized boat. The head of a swimmer is far more difficult for would-be rescuers to spot than is the larger hull, particularly at sea when the swimmer will disappear in the troughs of waves far more quickly and for longer than the upturned boat. Remember, too, that the shoreline always appears closer than it really is. It may seem to be within comfortable swimming distance and, indeed, if you were wearing suitable clothing it might be; encumbered by wet clothing and life-jacket or buoyancy aid the act of swimming becomes extremely difficult. There are also wind, currents and tides to be taken into account. Once having left the safety of the capsized boat it may be either difficult or impossible to return to it.

A further point about deserting a capsized boat is that it not only becomes a greater hazard to other craft than if there is someone beside or astride it to attract attention but it is also completely at the mercy of the elements and much more likely to be damaged. Even if they are not on board, a crew alongside an upturned craft can, for example, at least do something to protect it if it is being swept onto rocks or in to shore. Incidentally, a further point against boats with

Opposite:
A jib sheet provides a useful grip enabling the crew to put more weight into the righting moment – as the boat comes up, the helmsman will be scooped aboard.

Bottom:
Light boats with small cockpits like this Laster float so high it can be hard to get on to the centerboard.

extensive built-in buoyancy is that if the crews have to abandon efforts to right them and are holding on waiting for assistance, the fact that the hulls are riding high in the water makes them far more difficult to control in any way as they approach obstacles or inhospitable shores.

If the capsize has occurred at sea and the wind or tide is definitely carrying you away from the shore you should drop the anchor – both anchors if you are carrying two – at once. On the other hand, if you are drifting towards the shore and cannot right the boat without assistance it is as well to give yourself a chance to consider the situation. It may well be best to carry on drifting towards the coast at least until you are fairly close

in and then drop anchor. However, if you know that there are underwater obstructions such as rocks or hidden shoals which may cause damage to the boat, then drop anchor and, if you can, climb up on to the hull to await rescue.

Since we have placed some emphasis in this section on the subject of exhaustion this might be an appropriate place to consider the whole matter of physical fitness. Fitness is of general importance if you are going to sail well for any length of time and of particular importance if racing is the object. While it is essential to have the boat well tuned, it is just as important for the crew to be both physically and mentally well also, if success is to be achieved. There are certain injuries,

weaknesses or disabilities which will rule out sailing as a competitive sport or a relaxing hobby. Though strain on the heart and lungs is not as great as in, for example, rowing or athletics, anyone with cardiac or circulatory problems should consult a doctor before undertaking sailing. Similarly, anyone with a spinal weakness should take advice because sailing – particularly crewing – involves considerable strain on the spine to the extent that not only will an existing weakness be seriously aggravated but also that the act of sailing can itself cause spinal injuries.

Getting the best out of a boat and gaining the greatest enjoyment involves prolonged hard work and concentration; competing in races requires even more intensive concentration and physical activity. But both of these fall away rapidly if a person is not fit.

Obviously fitness is of the greatest importance when sailing single-handed, not just in the extreme cases of round-the-world or trans-oceanic single-handed sailing but also in the less dramatic circumstances of solo sailing in-shore or on inland waters. Once the lone sailor begins to feel the muscular twinges, cramps or draining away of energy he is in trouble and must hang on grimly or, in the extreme, call it a day and head for home.

In a two-man boat it is probable that the crew will begin to feel the effects sooner than the helmsman since to him, or her, falls the more strenuous job of leaning out or using the trapeze, both of which are extremely tiring. An experienced helmsman will learn to detect the signs of tiredness in his crew early on and should do all he can to ease the situation. He must also be ready to assert the authority of the skipper and insist that the crew does as he is told and does not, through pride, persist. The most tiring action of all is not, in fact, in using the trapeze, though this may appear to be so, but is in constant use of the toestraps. The helmsman himself has also to contend not only with controlling the boat but also with the tiring effects of prolonged concentration and decision-making.

If both crew and helmsman are suffering, the greatest danger is that their judgment will be so impaired that they do not realize just how fatigued they are. In such circumstances the helmsman may make disastrously wrong decisions and the crew, unable either to think or act quickly may move too slowly and be unable to correct the helmsman's mistake.

It will be as obvious to the watcher as it is to the participant that sailing involves a combination of sustained physical effort coupled with bursts of extreme exertion which do not usually last for very long; in racing, there is no time when helmsman or crew can afford to relax and take things easy.

As we have just mentioned, the business of

sitting out using the toestraps is more tiring than trapezing. Most involved are the muscles of the abdomen, the thigh, the upper and lower leg and the ankle. To a lesser extent, the muscles of the back, neck and arms are, of course, also employed. Whereas other maneuvers performed on board require positive or dynamic effort involving the various muscles contracting and relaxing, the act of sitting out using the toestraps or of using the trapeze involves a sustained static effort. That is to say that the muscles are made to adopt the correct position and remain there under contraction, without moving. Lack of training and fitness will quickly show itself because those muscles under the greatest strain will begin to tremble, then to shake quite violently, accompanied by an increasing pain which develops rapidly into excruciating discomfort and possibly cramp. The sufferer must abandon his position before the cramp stage is reached.

To become really fit it is necessary to strengthen the muscles to perform well dynamically and also under sustained contraction. If sailing is being undertaken only for pleasure, without thoughts of

Training and fitness are essential for even small sailboats.

competing and therefore putting the body to the greatest test, it is perfectly possible to achieve a sufficient degree of fitness by sailing regularly, starting with no more than half-an-hour on the water and gradually increasing the time and also the period during which you use toestraps or trapeze.

Ideally, though – and certainly when serious competition is involved – proper exercises are called for, first to bring yourself to fitness and then to maintain yourself in good trim. If this means indulging in more physical exertion than your body has been used to for some time, it is commonsense to start gradually with straightforward bending and stretching, relaxing and contracting exercises. These should be undertaken standing up and lying down. In addition, accustom your body to physical exertion by jogging or short-distance running.

Particular attention should be paid to exercising the spine by stretches, bends and rolls. An exercise which helps to correct a hollowed back is to lie down and press that part of the spine as hard as possible on to the floor while keeping both legs apart and both feet flat on the ground. This exercise will, when repeated over weeks and months, help to correct the tilting forward of the top of the pelvis which causes a hollow back. To begin with, press the hollowed part of the back against the floor only briefly, gradually extending the time by judging how you feel and eventually raising both legs off the ground as you use the abdominal muscles to straighten the spine. The duration of your exercise period can be increased steadily and as this is done you will notice that the abdominal muscles feel stronger and protest less.

If you are not able to take advantage of a gymnasium in which to exercise, it should be possible with a little ingenuity to devise a means whereby you can adopt a sitting out position at home. Start by lying on your back as before, with your legs apart and knees bent so that both feet are flat on the floor. Now sit up without using your arms as levers and without letting your feet come up. (It is harder than it sounds.) Repeat this several times and continue the exercise during your training sessions over the next few days, each time extending the period you remain in the position. Now you are ready for the next stage. A strong wide stool which is fairly low can be used as the gunwale and a fixed, low-down book shelf can be the toestraps. Sit on the stool, place your toes and about half of your foot under the shelf and ease yourself backwards off the seat until you are 'sitting out.' The ideal position is one in which the trunk and upper legs from a right angle and the upper and lower legs form another right angle at the knees. The lower legs and the feet make a third right angle and the heels and buttocks are just about horizontally level.

It can be appreciated that to maintain this position for some time requires the use also of the thigh muscles which must be trained to remain static under tension. There is a difference in building a dynamic muscle which is to be used essentially for movement and training a static muscle to accept prolonged contraction. The first requires intensive movement carried out in short bursts of activity; the second involves slower, more rhythmic movement which steadily gets the muscle used to longer usage. Start off by extending the arms straight in front of you and standing on one leg. Slowly bend that leg as you bring the other straight up in front of you. Go down until from knee to buttock your thigh is approximately parallel with the floor. Repeat standing on the other leg.

If you have weights use these across your shoulders to do knee-bend exercises, keeping your back straight and going down to the same position as before without raising your heels. Do not attempt to lift too great a weight to begin with: about one-quarter to one-third of your body weight is sufficient at first. Nor should you overstrain yourself by attempting more than about a dozen bends before resting. Then increasing the weight and, having become used to that, extend the number of bends. Always try to work both slowly and smoothly, not in quick jerks.

These exercises with the weights are excellent for toestrap training. By slightly altering them they also become suitable for acquainting you with trapeze work: simply bend the leg that much further so that your buttocks touch your heels – which still must not be raised. Get used to that position and gradually increase the *pace* of the bending and stretching since this is a dynamic exercise rather than training for static work. Again, having become used to the weight, speed and new position, increase the weight and then the speed of the movements progressively. Do not attempt to lift more than 75 to 80 percent of your own bodyweight and do not forget to rest between each series of exercises.

When doing the 'toestrap' exercises you can complete a dozen bends and then rest for at least half-a-minute – and for at least two minutes at first. However, when carrying out the 'trapeze' movements do not do more than three movements at the heaviest weight before resting for 30 seconds, then doing three more, resting again for 30 seconds and finally a third series of three before a complete break.

It should be emphasized again that these exercises should not be undertaken without first having a proper medical examination. If, at any stage of the build-up in your program of exercise, you feel any undue strain or palpitations – stop and, if you are concerned, take advice from your doctor.

Beach boats like this Hobie Cat may tempt sailors not to wear a buoyancy aid, but it is always sensible to do so. Few catamarans may be righted easily; note again the use of a rope to give leverage.

A Bermudan Cutter and a Freedom 40 sail off Rhode Island.

8 IN TUNE

A fleet of modern offshore yachts starting a race in the Solent.

The more experienced a sailor becomes the greater will be his awareness of how well or how poorly a boat is performing and the greater his desire will become to have a well-tuned boat.

To achieve this happy state he must know how to adjust the 'sailing parts' of the boat so that each is working to maximum efficiency and none is working in opposition. In addition to knowing how to make adjustments he needs to know why they will make a difference to the way the boat performs. That, in turn, involves learning a bit more about the theory of sailing.

Ideally, tuning the boat should be carried out on a calm day when there is a light breeze blowing. The helmsman should choose a stretch of water where there are no conflicting currents which might tend to give a false impression of the way the craft is performing.

In these conditions he sails the boat close-hauled with the sheets hardened in and the centerboard lowered right down. Now he observes the behavior of the boat and of the sails. The jib, for example, should not spill air on to the mainsail, causing it to lift. If this happens – it is described as the jib backwinding the mainsail – the helmsman should sheet the mainsail in still farther. As he does so he may find that the boat either tries to come up into the wind and can be felt resisting efforts to bring her back, or it behaves in an opposite manner and can be felt wanting to bear away from the wind.

In the first case, with the boat trying to turn into the wind, it is carrying weather helm; in the second it carries lee helm. With a weather helm the boat is unable to develop maximum speed because the rudder is not in line with the centerline and is having a significant braking effect

Sailing close hauled. The boat is on too even a keel, hence the slight weather helm. Note the finger-tip control of the tiller.

Top left:
Lasers tune up against each other in an ideal wind.

Top right:
A Cherub sailboat planes under spinnaker; she is slightly out of balance and the pressure on the helm will be considerable.

on forward movement of the boat.

If the mainsail is eased a little at the same time as the jib is also eased, the boat should gather speed again, pointing a little farther off the wind. If it does not and still shows signs of a weather helm the answer may be in adjusting the centerboard. If this is raised the boat should now come a few points off the wind and be gathering speed as she had been expected to do before. She will be heeling at only about five degrees and sailing quite steadily.

Now let go of the tiller. If she again shoots up into the wind she is still carrying a weather helm and the previous adjustments have not cured that situation. The problem is that the center of effort is aft of the center of lateral resistance instead of the two being in perfect balance.

In theory if the boat is to move forward in a straight line at a constant speed the center of the propelling forces and the center of the forces which are resisting its forward motion must come together.

The position of the center of effort, which is the point through which the aerodynamic force acts, depends upon the type of sails being used, their shape and their trim, the rake of the mast and the heel of the boat. For example, if the spinnaker is hoisted the aerodynamic force will tend to be concentrated further forward, where the greater sail area is presented. The center of effort is, thus moved forward.

The position of the center of lateral resistance, which is the point through which the hydro-dynamic force acts, depends mainly upon the speed of the boat. The faster the boat moves, the farther forward is the center of lateral resistance. As it slows down the center of lateral resistance moves aft and if the boat goes backwards (makes sternway) it goes right aft. With a small boat the center of lateral resistance can be altered by

using the centerboard: the farther down the centerboard is, the farther forward is the center; if it is raised, the center is moved aft.

Returning to the boat which is exhibiting signs of carrying a weather helm, there are a number of possible adjustments which can be made in addition to those we have mentioned and which did not work in this theoretical case. Remember that the center of effort is too far aft. To get perfect balance we must therefore either move it forward or bring the center of lateral resistance the same distance aft as well.

The centerboard can be lifted slightly to achieve this latter effect but that is really only a temporary measure and would mean that the

This boat suffers from some weather helm, possibly because the sail is too full. The outhaul should be tightened.

Even strict one-designs sail at different speeds – proper tuning will not get you to the front but it will ensure you are not at a disadvantage.

Top:
A well-set jib on this 505 sailboat. The telltales sited 6-8 in behind the luff are a useful guide to sheeting. They should run horizontally and lift at the same time.

Opposite:
The kicking strap prevents the boom lifting on a close reach and letting excessive twist into the mainsail so reducing power.

adjusting the wedging to give equal play.

A further reason for the imbalance may be less obvious: it may be caused by unequal flexibility along the whole length of the mast, though this is much less likely in metal masts than in those made by bonding two sections of wood together. This method of mast-making involves two pieces of wood being glued together in such a way that the grain on each runs in opposite directions. It requires only a slight difference in the graining of the two pieces to bring about a difference in the flexing characteristics of the two. Thus, on one tack the mast may bend smoothly, while on the other it is more rigid. (If such a failing is exhibited in a metal mast the answer can only lie in a serious fault in the metal and there would be fair grounds for insisting on a free replacement from the makers.)

Imbalance in flexibility of the mast can be treated though it is unlikely to be entirely cured. The answer lies in fitting a 'diamond' – a pair of rigid short spreaders on either side of the mast. A thin steel wire is lead across each and stretched taut from the hounds to the foot of the mast, where they are attached. It will be appreciated that the tensioning of the wires equalizes the flexing of the mast to a considerable degree.

There is a further means of curing the weather helm on which we started this section – though it will depend, in competition, on the class rules covering the type of boat involved. The tack of the jib fitting can be moved forward so that the aerodynamic force on this sail's area is working further in front of the mast, bringing the center of effort forward.

If the boat has shown that she is carrying lee helm the answer lies in doing the reverse of what you do to cure a weather helm. In other words, the foot of the mast can be moved aft to shift the center of effort back; the centerplate can be lowered farther (if it is not already fully down) or consideration can be given, in the extreme, to shifting the whole fitting forward to move the center of lateral resistance; the tack fitting of the jib can be brought slightly aft.

A well-set jib can be spotted at once because its luff will lift along its full length as soon as the boat is slightly luffed up, without any signs of shaking unevenly. It will be a smooth filling. However, if the luff shows a tendency to lift along its lower edge first, the sheet leads are probably too far forward and should be moved aft and refixed. If lifting starts in the upper part, the leads are too far aft and should be taken forward. If the jib is seen to be shaking along its leech, even when it is sheeted hard in, the leads are too far aft and should be adjusted.

One of the first steps in tuning a boat to perfection is to make sure that the sails set well. This will depend on a number of variables such as the

centerboard could never be fully lowered. To bring about a permanent cure through the centerboard would involve moving the whole fitting slightly aft and this becomes a fairly major operation not to be undertaken lightly.

However, there is a less drastic cure: the foot of the mast can be moved forward in its step to adjust the center of effort, making sure that the recommended rake of between 15 and 30 thousandths which you previously determined is not altered.

In fact, the mast is arguably the most sensitive part of the whole boat and as such, particular attention should be paid to it when the boat is being tuned. For example, it may well be that the boat shows itself to be carrying weather helm on one tack but on the other it may show exactly the opposite effect and carry lee helm. In these circumstances it may be that the crosstrees up the mast are of unequal length or the shrouds are not equal – or are wrongly tensioned. On the other hand it may be that the trouble lies at deck level where the mast has greater lateral movement one way than the other. This is simply a matter of

flexibility of the mast, tension of shrouds and halyard, positioning of sheet leads, all of which have an effect on the angle that the sails make in relation to the wind. What cannot be counted as a variable is the actual shape of the sails themselves since these are cut to pattern. However, their shape has a considerable influence on the tuning of the boat because it will determine the extent to which their curvature can be adjusted in relation to the strength of the wind.

The curve of a sail will always be approximately in its center in a light breeze. As the wind increases in strength the curve moves further aft if it is not controlled. It is brought back to the middle by hardening the sail – tightening the luff. The other thing that should happen as the strength of the wind increases is that the sails should be flattened more so that the area of the curve does not become too great. The act of flattening the sail deflects the air at a smaller, more effective angle. The position of the curve is controlled by tension on the luff while the degree of curvature is determined by use of luff tension and kicking strap or vang.

So far as the jib is concerned, its curve cannot be controlled if the sail has a wire luff but if the luff is of rope the sail can be stretched like the mainsail.

The mainsail will normally always want to take up a twisted, helicoidal shape. This is because the top of the sail is less restricted than the foot, which is held by the boom. The head therefore tends to turn into line with the wind. Though a limited amount of twist is not necessarily detrimental so long as it is controlled, with a following wind the twist can become dangerous. Unless the downhaul is tightened sufficiently to flatten the sail, the boat will luff and heel sharply to wind-

ward. The helmsman will then have to bear away repeatedly to correct and in doing so will find that the boat becomes difficult to control because it starts to roll.

The kicking strap or American vang is used close-hauled to modify the curvature of the sail by bending the boom and the mast and it also provides a means of controlling the twist of the sail. Even on boats fitted with a traveller the kicking strap is useful on points of sailing which require the sail to be eased so far out that the traveller can no longer be used. Except in those circumstances, however, the traveller is a more efficient means of flattening the sail and controlling the twist.

From all that has been said it is obvious that the best performance can only be achieved if the sails are kept carefully trimmed all the time in relation to the angle of the apparent wind. Remember that the apparent wind is the combination of the effects of the true wind and the wind created by the movement of the boat in any direction. If a boat sails dead before the true wind, the all-important apparent wind is considerably less than the true wind because the wind of its own speed is working in exactly the opposite direction and must be subtracted from the value of the true wind. If we express true wind as WT, wind of the boat's own speed as WS and apparent wind as WA the equation in these circumstances is: $WA = WT - WS$.

In theory a boat performs best when the sails are trimmed to an angle of 22 degrees to the apparent wind. That angle is determined by taking the chord of the curvature of the sail at the height of the center of effort. The ideal is to maintain that angle when sailing close-hauled so that the sails are fully efficient and to do so involves constant re-trimming and alterations of course since the wind is always changing in speed and direction, even if only minutely.

Apart from the repeated trimming of the sails

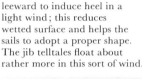

The crew of this Star sits to leeward to induce heel in a light wind; this reduces wetted surface and helps the sails to adopt a proper shape. The jib telltales float about rather more in this sort of wind.

in relation to the angle of the apparent wind, trimming is also used to minimize heeling because most boats perform best when heeling as little as possible. Too much heel induces a weather helm and also means that the part of the hull specifically designed to carve through the water is not given a chance to work at its peak of efficiency.

In fact no boat will give of its best if it is not allowed to float in the water in the way its designer intended. This applies as much to its fore-and-aft trim as to its lateral trim. So far as the former is concerned, the helmsman should try to ensure that the weight is concentrated as close to the middle of the boat as possible. This is particularly important in some very small sailboats but also applies to yachts and cruisers in which the helmsman can detect with his eyes shut when someone has moved forward or aft by a change in the handling characteristics of the boat.

In a small sailboat the effects of wrong weight distribution are exaggerated because of its size.

If the crew (in the collective sense of both the helmsman and crewman) are so positioned that the center of their combined weight is too far forward, the bow will tend to dig in and the rudder will be too high to perform efficiently; if it is too far aft, the boat will sail nose up and be sluggish to handle. In each case the boat will pitch far more on rough water than if the weight was concentrated at or near the middle.

It is not, of course, possible to make a hard and fast rule about this, for boats and people are all different and have to be treated differently. In addition, the crew has to move about to give the boat its maximum efficiency as well as to perform various maneuvers. Though the sails can be trimmed to reduce heeling and assist lateral trim, the crew also plays an important part as we have seen.

In any tuning run it is a good idea for the crew to discover the effects which sitting out to a greater or less degree have upon the boat when she is on various courses. He will soon discover that it is far better to sit out *before* the boat starts to take on an acute heel; he should anticipate and sit out while it is still almost upright rather than wait until it is already well over, by which time it will be more difficult for him to have as great an effect in helping to trim the boat.

The crew will also find that, certainly in most boats, a small amount of heel in light weather is a good thing. Not only does it help to keep the sails to leeward; it also reduces drag on the hull because the wetted area is less.

The helmsman of this Laser has moved right forward to lift the flat after section out of the water and reduce wetted surface.

Journey's end for this Atlantic voyager. Past Europa Point lighthouse, Gibraltar, lies the Mediterranean.

9 GETTING YOUR BEARINGS

Cutter-rigged *Elka* in convoy with *Moody 39* production cruiser in the Solent.

Though the majority of small-boat sailors will not normally need to use a compass it is a good idea to learn how to use one and how to get one's bearings. You never know when a compass is likely to come in handy and it is also fair to assume that many of the small-boat sailors will graduate to sailing larger boats on which the knowledge will be invaluable.

Essentially a bearing is the direction of one object from another. It can be given as true, magnetic or relative to the course of the boat from which it is taken. In the latter form, the object on which a bearing is being taken could be referred to as 'ahead' (in front of the bow), 'on the port bow' (left of the bow), 'on the port beam' (about 90 degrees from the bow), 'on the port quarter' (aft of the port beam but not behind the stern of the boat), and 'astern' (behind the boat, beyond its stern). On the right of the boat the bearings would be starboard bow, starboard beam and starboard quarter.

A more general and less specific 'bearing' can be given by saying that an object is 'to windward' which means simply that it is in the direction from which the wind is blowing, or 'to leeward,' which places it on the side away from the wind. But this is so imprecise as to give rise to confusion or lost time in searching for the object.

A compass is obviously the most precise means of determining your position in relation to magnetic North and in taking an accurate bearing on an object in relation to your own position. There are many different types of compass but all work on the same principle. Basically each compass consists of a compass card on which the points or 360 degrees of the compass are marked and to which a magnetic needle is fixed. The center of the card has a bearing which allows it to rotate freely on a pivot inside the compass bowl, which is filled with liquid – petroleum spirit, glycerine, white spirit or water and alcohol.

The compass is housed in a binnacle and is suspended on gimbals (or gymbals) which enable it to maintain a horizontal position by countering the movement of the vessel.

There are various types of compass. The *traditional* is the simplest but it is difficult for a helmsman to read because it only has small graduation marks. The *domed*, which has a magnifying dome over the traditional compass, enables readings to be taken more easily but it is not ideal for a tiller-steered boat. The *grid steering* compass has the centerline, or lubberline, of the boat clearly marked on the card and continued onto the outside of the bowl. The glass has a transparent grid superimposed and marked from 0° to 360° and two parallel north-south lines. The grid can be rotated and locked in position, when the selected course coincides with the lubberline. The helmsman then aligns the north-south line on the compass card with the middle of the grid lines.

Another version of the grid steering compass dispenses with the transparent grid. The north-south lines are marked on the glass while the rim of the compass bowl carries the grid. The whole compass turns in a frame carrying a lubberline. A drawback to the first type of grid steering compass can be that condensation between the glass and the superimposed grid can cause difficulty in reading; with the second type you cannot read off the course without lining up the zero mark of the bowl with the lubberline on the ring.

A hand-bearing compass is a simpler, smaller version which, as the name implies, is held in the hand, the user siting by holding it horizontally and viewing the compass card through a prism while still being able to see the object on which he is obtaining a bearing directly over the compass.

Since it is portable, a hand-bearing compass is not compensated and is affected by metal objects including the hulls of boats constructed of steel or ferro-cement. The other types of compass we have mentioned are all installed as fixtures and can be compensated. It is, of course, best to install a compass so that it is as far as possible from anything metal on a boat but this is not always possible and some deviation is to be expected. Compensation should then be carried out by an expert who

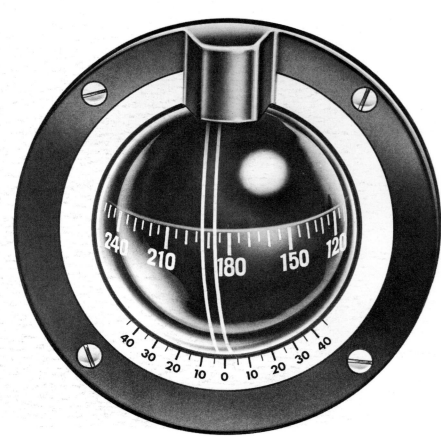

A porthole-type compass suitable for fitting in a bulkhead; the lubberline read against the low figures indicates the angle of heel.

will know exactly where to place the magnets used to counteract the deviation caused by magnetic influences. If a metal object on board causes the card to swing, for example, four degrees away from magnetic north, he will place a magnet of the right strength and in the correct position to bring the card back those four points. This, of course, works for magnetic objects which are a *fixed* influence but not for any which are movable and care should be taken not to place portable metal objects near a fixed compass.

A point to watch in this context is the way in which the compass is lit. If it is equipped with built-in lighting there should be no problem but a do-it-yourself lighting system requires thought. The safest method is to wire a bulb into the boat's electrical supply. If batteries are being used it is important to ensure that they are anti-magnetic or that, if not, they are kept away from the compass. Even though a battery may be claimed by its makers to be anti-magnetic the casing may not be perfect. Flashlight batteries can be easily checked by placing them individually over the compass. If there is any reaction on the card the battery should not be used in a flashlight for illuminating the compass.

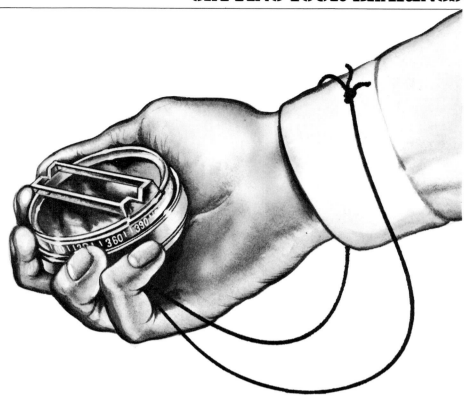

Top:
A small hand-bearing compass. The object is lined up with the sights and the bearing read off below the near sight.

Bottom:
Using a larger hand-bearing compass.

The compass is part of the basic navigation equipment which should also include a log, charts and measuring equipment (ruler, dividers, protractors) and on larger boats a barometer, leadline, sextant and radio.

The simplest log is the original 'ships log' which consists of a flat piece of wood weighted to float upright and attached to a line which is payed out astern. The inventor of the log is not known and it does not appear to have been mentioned before 1607, when its use is recorded in the published report of an East India voyage. Before that it was very common to throw overboard a log or piece of wood from as far forward as possible and then for a member of the crew to keep pace with it by walking aft until it passed the stern. In this way the speed of the boat could be estimated with remarkable accuracy. Since lumps of wood were

not in inexhaustible supply aboard ship it seems likely that someone had the idea of tethering the log and dividing the line into equal sections marked off with knots.

In 1867 the *Sailor's Word-Book* by Admiral W H Smyth described the log-line as being about 100 fathoms long (one fathom equals six feet or 1.8m), fastened to the 'log-ship' by means of two legs, one of which passed through a hole in the corner and knotted while the other was attached by a pin which drew out when the sand-glass used to time the rate ran out (usually after 28 or 14 seconds). The line had 'certain knots or divisions, which ought to be 47ft 4in [14.4m] from each other though it was common practice not to have them above 42ft [12.8m] . . . . For so many knots run out, so many miles the ship sails in an hour,' the Admiral recorded.

Bottom:
A well-equipped navigation area can resemble an aircraft console. Notice also the chart table below with chart and parallel rule in use.

Opposite:
Using a sextant; even near land it can be a useful tool.

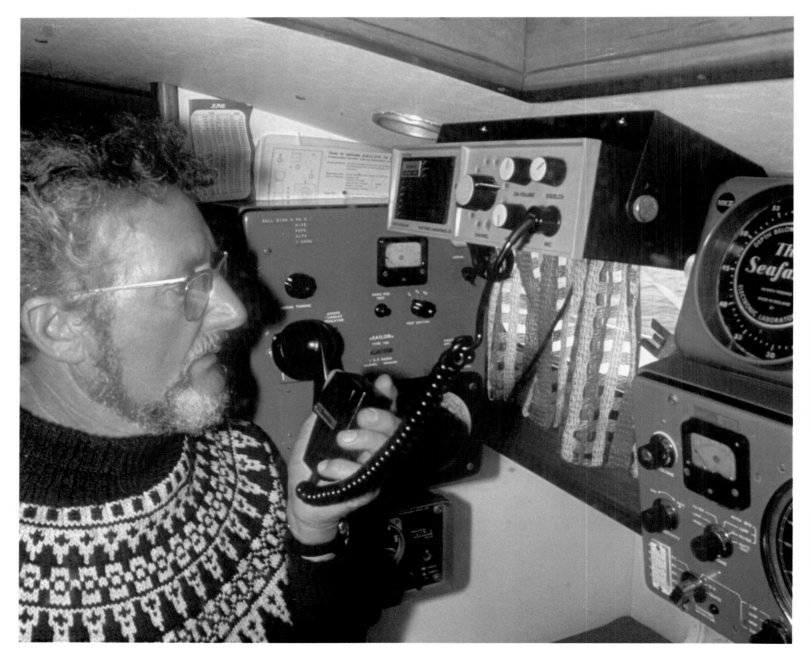

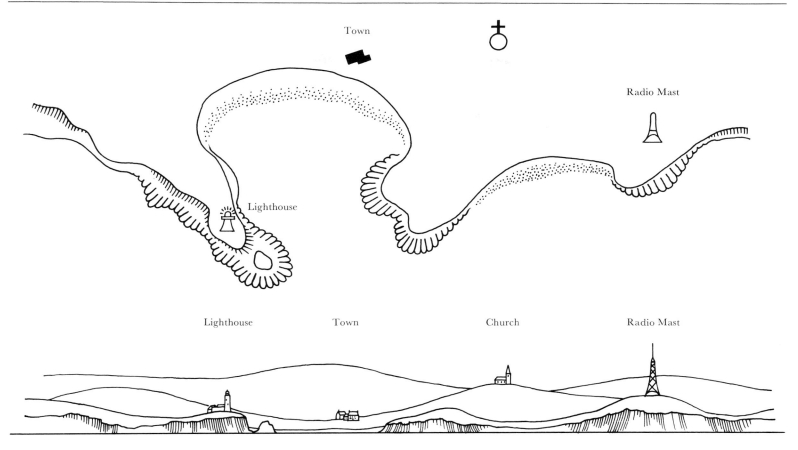

Town

Radio Mast

Lighthouse

Lighthouse   Town   Church   Radio Mast

Nowadays such a log is usually made with knots 25ft 4in (7.71m which is 1/240 of a nautical mile) apart. After the log is dropped overboard and the first knot has been payed out, 15 seconds (1/240 of an hour) are allowed to elapse and the knots counted. Each knot in the water equals one nautical mile per hour.

One modern version of the old 'ships log' is the patent log or mechanical log, which consists of a graduated meter which records the distance travelled by means of a rotator which is spun by the movement of the water over it. It does not work well at low speeds – say, less than about two knots. Even more sophisticated and expensive, the electronic log consists also of a rotator which, rather than being streamed, is fixed to the hull and counts its revolutions (converted into distance and speed) electronically.

Navigation is, to quote Admiral Smyth once more, 'the art of conducting vessels on the sea, not only by the peculiar knowledge of seamanship in all its intricate details, but also by such a knowledge of the higher branches of nautical astronomy as enables the commander to hit his port, after a long succession of bad weather, and an absence of three or four months from all land. Any man without science may navigate the entire canals of Great Britain, but may be unable to pass from Plymouth to Guernsey.'

In normal small-sailboat sailing, navigation in that sense, making use of instruments, never arises. However, once a boat has ventured from the shore 'the peculiar knowledge of seamanship' is required in some degree to ensure a safe return.

That, in itself, implies a basic knowledge of navigation: in knowing how to use landmarks, how to choose the best tacks to get back to port, what obstacles there may be between boat and shore, what the tide and local currents are doing and so on.

Generally one can gain sufficient knowledge of the local conditions, rocks, sandbanks, tides and so on by talking to the harbormaster, coastguard or to other sailors who know the area. It is not a bad idea to try to get a look at a chart showing the area but it should not be necessary to go to the length of buying one. Nonetheless, if we continue with our assumption that many smaller boat sailors will graduate to larger boats at some time – and are at least likely to have the opportunity of crewing on a day's sailing – it is no bad thing to learn at least the basics of true navigation. With the increasing availability of boats for hire - particularly cruisers – there has been a comparable increase in the number of people who think that it is safe to leave harbor with a good stock of food and drink, plenty of enthusiasm and nothing else. The work of the lifeboat men would be made that much easier if all sailors were equipped with commonsense, basic navigational knowledge and – if anything more than a trip round the bay is planned – the necessary charts and complementary equipment.

It takes very little effort, for example, for everyone on board, not just the skipper, to study the outline of the shore from which they are departing and to which they intend to return. They should make at least a mental note of any obvious land-

Top:
Visualizing land from a chart takes experience – buildings, preferably tall and distinctive, are most useful. The lie of the land can be deceptive; notice here how the bay is lost from seaward.

Opposite:
The welcome lighthouse at Plymouth breakwater.

marks such as high points, church towers, breakwaters, factory chimneys, clusters of rocks, particular buoys and, of course, lighthouses. There may also be certain rocks which have been deliberately painted white as navigational aids.

That alone is not enough. If a cruise along the coast and back is planned, those aboard should take similar note of landmarks along the way. One small coastal village can look exactly like another even in good visibility; if bad visibility has come down and the light is fading, the job of identifying the right one can become surprisingly difficult.

The selection and memorizing of particular landmarks should be only the start. On board there should also be the right chart or charts to cover the area over which it is planned to cruise or sail. The skipper should also know where any lights, foghorns or whistles are positioned and what the depth of the water will be at any and all times of day. To know that, and what the various tidal streams are doing, he must study the charts, Pilot books and the *Admiralty List of Lights and Tide Tables*. The various land and sea marks are listed in a variety of official reference works in all marine countries: in Britain the information can be gained from the Admiralty Pilots and *Reed's Almanac*; in France it is found in *Renseignements Relatifs aux Documents Nautique et à la Navigation* while the equivalent in the United States would be *Coast Pilots of the Oceanographic Office*. The charts are published by the Admiralty and by various nautical publishers throughout the world.

Coastal charts combine the markings found on normal land maps for landmarks such as churches, lighthouses, hills, trees, etc, with information about the larger area of sea occupying most of the 'map': the depths, positions of rocks, shoals, buoys, lights and so on.

The depths, which are known as soundings, marked on a chart are the depths below the Chart Datum. The datum line is the level to which soundings are reduced on any one chart because the tide is unlikely ever to fall below it. Therefore, the actual depth of the water at any point is obtained by adding the charted depth to the height of the tide at the time. However, if the depth figure on the chart has a line ruled beneath it, this means that the seabed rises that much above the Chart Datum. In that case the true depth is the height of the tide *minus* the figure on the chart.

Obviously it is important to know this since the sailor who cheerfully believes that the depths shown on a chart apply all the time and are actual depths is going to be in all kinds of trouble. Equally, it is important to know that the tide does not ebb or flow at a steady rate. After reaching high tide or high water there is a short pause and then the water begins to fall, slowly at first but

increasing its rate for just over three hours, when half tide is reached. Thereafter the rate of ebb begins to slow until, after a further three hours and a few minutes, the speed of the water running out and the rate of ebb slows right down until it again pauses at low water or low tide before starting to flood in once more. Again, the rate of the flooding tide gradually increases to a peak at half tide after about three hours before decreasing and passing at high water.

The times of high and low water are not the same each day, nor are the extent of the rise and fall of the water identical. Each varies according to the relative positions of the moon, the sun and the earth. A spring tide (when the range between rise and fall is at its maximum and the highest tides occur in the Western hemisphere) comes when the sun and moon are in conjunction or in opposition – that is, approximately in line viewed from the earth. This happens just after a full moon or a new moon, in other words, once every two weeks and has nothing to do with the season of spring. The further out of alignment the sun and moon move, the less becomes the range of the tide so that the small, neap tides come during the period when they have moved most out of line in the first and last quarters of the moon. Then the water at high tide is at its lowest and at low tide is at its highest, since it is not pulled out by the sun and moon as much as at the time of spring tides. The range of the tides also varies from one month to the next and at the time of the spring and autumn equinoxes is at its greatest. To complicate matters still further the range of the equinoctial tides is not constant from one year to the next.

It is important to appreciate that the height of the tide given in the tide tables is *not* the depth of the water at any particular point. That, as we have said, is measured from the Chart Datum plus the height of the tide. A further point to be noted is that whatever the range of the tide at a given spot (whether it is the time of a spring tide or a neap tide), *the depth of the sea is always the same at half tide* and this is called the mean level.

The tide tables in Britain will show the times of high water at various recognized ports, the heights at high water, the mean level at the standard ports and at some secondary ports and tables which enable navigators to work out the state of the tide at any hour. This information is also given in the tide tables of most other countries. However, in France they include additional useful information in the form of a table of coefficients for each tide of the year. This indicates the size of the tide, dependent upon the position of the sun and moon on any one day in the year.

The coefficient is given in terms of hundredths, with 20 representing the lowest known tides, 45 the average neap tides, 70 the average tides, 95 the average spring tides and 120 the highest tide.

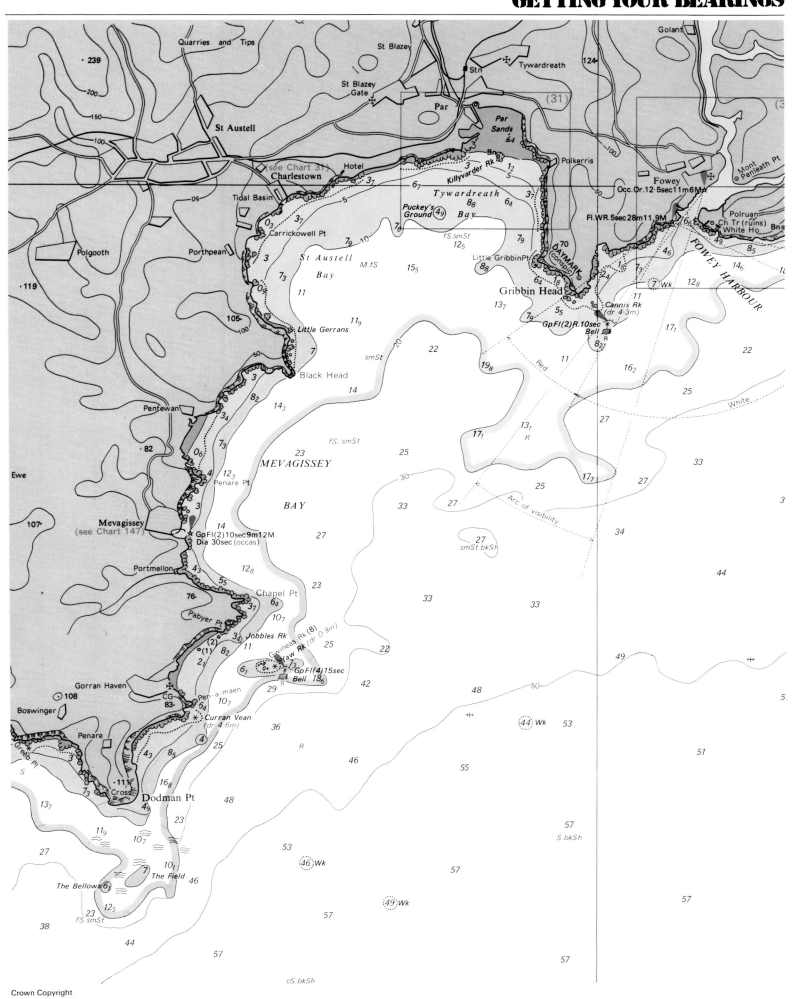

Crown Copyright

PORTSMOUTH

G.M.T. ADD 1 HOUR MARCH 19-OCTOBER 29 FOR B.S.T.

JANUARY

Date	Time h.min.	Ht. m.	Time h.min.	Ht. m.	Time h.min.	Ht. m.	Time h.min.	Ht. m.
1 Su	0318	4.3	0821	1.4	1527	4.1	2042	1.2
2 M	0402	4.2	0910	1.5	1618	4.0	2137	1.3
3 Tu	0457	4.1	1012	1.5	1721	3.9	2244	1.5
4 W	0602	4.1	1125	1.5	1835	4.0	—	—
5 Th	0000	1.5	0712	4.2	1239	1.4	1949	4.1
6 F	0112	1.3	0818	4.4	1347	1.1	2056	4.4
7 Sa	0215	1.1	0921	4.6	1449	0.9	2157	4.6
8 Su	0313	0.9	1018	4.8	1544	0.7	2253	4.8
9 M	0406	0.7	1112	4.9	1634	0.5	2345	4.9
10 Tu	0453	0.6	1201	4.9	1721	0.5	—	—
11 W	0033	4.9	0539	0.7	1246	4.8	1806	0.5
12 Th	0119	4.9	0624	0.8	1329	4.7	1849	0.6
13 F	0205	4.9	0709	0.9	1413	4.5	1935	0.8
14 Sa	0252	4.8	0755	1.1	1500	4.5	2022	1.0
15 Su	0340	4.6	0846	1.3	1550	4.3	2115	1.3
16 M	0432	4.4	0942	1.5	1650	4.0	2214	1.6
17 Tu	0531	4.1	1049	1.7	1800	3.8	2325	1.8
18 W	0636	4.0	1204	1.7	1918	3.8	—	—
19 Th	0039	1.8	0745	3.9	1315	1.6	2029	3.8
20 F	0144	1.7	0845	4.0	1414	1.5	2126	4.0
21 Sa	0235	1.6	0935	4.2	1502	1.3	2212	4.2
22 Su	0317	1.4	1019	4.3	1541	1.1	2249	4.3
23 M	0354	1.2	1056	4.4	1615	1.0	2322	4.4
24 Tu	0428	1.0	1130	4.4	1648	0.9	2353	4.4
25 W	0501	1.0	1201	4.4	1719	0.8	—	—
26 Th	0025	4.4	0535	0.9	1234	4.3	1752	0.8
27 F	0059	4.4	0609	0.9	1309	4.3	1825	0.7
28 Sa	0136	4.4	0643	0.9	1346	4.3	1900	0.7
29 Su	0215	4.4	0718	0.9	1424	4.3	1937	0.7
30 M	0254	4.4	0755	1.0	1506	4.2	2017	0.9
31 Tu	0336	4.3	0838	1.1	1552	4.1	2105	1.1

FEBRUARY

Date	Time h.min.	Ht. m.	Time h.min.	Ht. m.	Time h.min.	Ht. m.	Time h.min.	Ht. m.
1 W	0424	4.2	0933	1.3	1650	4.0	2208	1.4
2 Th	0526	4.0	1047	1.5	1805	3.9	2328	1.6
3 F	0642	4.0	1211	1.4	1930	4.0	—	—
4 Sa	0051	1.5	0759	4.2	1330	1.2	2045	4.2
5 Su	0202	1.2	0906	4.4	1436	0.9	2148	4.4
6 M	0301	0.9	1006	4.6	1532	0.7	2243	4.7
7 Tu	0353	0.7	1059	4.7	1622	0.5	2332	4.8
8 W	0440	0.6	1147	4.8	1707	0.4	—	—
9 Th	0017	4.9	0525	0.5	1229	4.8	1749	0.4
10 F	0101	4.9	0607	0.6	1311	4.8	1830	0.5
11 Sa	0143	4.8	0648	0.7	1352	4.7	1910	0.7
12 Su	0224	4.8	0728	0.9	1436	4.6	1950	0.9
13 M	0304	4.6	0811	1.1	1517	4.4	2034	1.2
14 Tu	0346	4.4	0857	1.3	1607	4.1	2125	1.5
15 W	0434	4.1	0944	1.6	1708	3.8	2229	1.8
16 Th	0537	3.8	1107	1.8	1826	3.6	2349	2.0
17 F	0654	3.7	1230	1.8	1950	3.6	—	—
18 Sa	0108	1.9	0808	3.7	1344	1.7	2058	3.8
19 Su	0211	1.7	0909	3.9	1438	1.4	2148	4.0
20 M	0256	1.4	0957	4.1	1518	1.2	2226	4.2
21 Tu	0334	1.2	1035	4.2	1553	1.0	2258	4.4
22 W	0406	1.0	1108	4.3	1624	0.8	2328	4.4
23 Th	0439	0.8	1139	4.4	1657	0.7	—	—
24 F	0000	4.5	0513	0.8	1211	4.4	1732	0.6
25 Sa	0034	4.5	0549	0.7	1247	4.5	1808	0.5
26 Su	0112	4.6	0624	0.6	1327	4.5	1844	0.5
27 M	0153	4.6	0700	0.6	1408	4.5	1920	0.5
28 Tu	0233	4.5	0737	0.7	1451	4.4	1959	0.7

MARCH

Date	Time h.min.	Ht. m.	Time h.min.	Ht. m.	Time h.min.	Ht. m.	Time h.min.	Ht. m.
1 W	0314	4.4	0818	0.9	1537	4.2	2045	1.0
2 Th	0401	4.2	0911	1.2	1634	4.0	2147	1.4
3 F	0503	4.0	1024	1.4	1751	3.8	—	—
4 Sa	0624	3.9	1155	1.5	1922	3.8	—	—
5 Su	0040	1.6	0748	4.0	1319	1.3	2038	4.1
6 M	0153	1.3	0856	4.2	1425	1.0	2139	4.4
7 Tu	0252	1.0	0953	4.4	1520	0.6	2230	4.6
8 W	0341	0.7	1043	4.6	1607	0.4	2316	4.7
9 Th	0425	0.5	1128	4.7	1650	0.3	2359	4.8
10 F	0507	0.5	1211	4.7	1730	0.4	—	—
11 Sa	0039	4.8	0547	0.5	1251	4.7	1809	0.5
12 Su	0118	4.8	0624	0.6	1331	4.7	1845	0.6
13 M	0154	4.7	0701	0.7	1410	4.6	1919	0.9
14 Tu	0229	4.6	0736	0.9	1449	4.4	1957	1.2
15 W	0305	4.4	0817	1.2	1531	4.1	2040	1.5
16 Th	0346	4.1	0906	1.5	1623	3.8	2137	1.8
17 F	0440	3.8	1011	1.8	1732	3.6	2253	2.0
18 Sa	0556	3.6	1135	1.9	1858	3.5	2310	1.6
19 Su	0022	2.0	0722	3.5	1259	1.8	2016	3.6
20 M	0134	1.8	0833	3.7	1401	1.5	2111	3.9
21 Tu	0226	1.5	0924	3.9	1444	1.2	2153	4.1
22 W	0305	1.2	1005	4.1	1520	1.0	2227	4.3
23 Th	0338	1.0	1038	4.3	1554	0.7	2259	4.5
24 F	0412	0.8	1110	4.5	1630	0.6	2332	4.6
25 Sa	0447	0.6	1146	4.6	1709	0.5	—	—
26 Su	0009	4.7	0525	0.5	1226	4.6	1747	0.4
27 M	0049	4.7	0604	0.4	1308	4.6	1827	0.4
28 Tu	0130	4.7	0643	0.4	1353	4.6	1904	0.5
29 W	0213	4.6	0723	0.5	1439	4.5	1945	0.7
30 Th	0256	4.4	0807	0.8	1528	4.3	2032	1.1
31 F	0346	4.2	0901	1.1	1628	4.0	2135	1.4

APRIL

Date	Time h.min.	Ht. m.	Time h.min.	Ht. m.	Time h.min.	Ht. m.	Time h.min.	Ht. m.
1 Sa	0450	3.9	1013	1.4	1747	3.8	2300	1.6
2 Su	0614	3.8	1144	1.5	1915	3.9	—	—
3 M	0030	1.5	0738	3.9	1307	1.3	2028	4.1
4 Tu	0142	1.3	0845	4.1	1410	1.0	2125	4.4
5 W	0237	1.0	0938	4.3	1501	0.7	2211	4.6
6 Th	0324	0.8	1024	4.5	1546	0.5	2254	4.7
7 F	0406	0.6	1106	4.6	1629	0.5	2335	4.7
8 Sa	0446	0.5	1149	4.7	1708	0.5	—	—
9 Su	0013	4.7	0524	0.5	1229	4.7	1745	0.5
10 M	0050	4.7	0600	0.6	1310	4.6	1819	0.7
11 Tu	0125	4.6	0634	0.7	1348	4.5	1850	0.9
12 W	0157	4.5	0707	0.9	1424	4.4	1923	1.2
13 Th	0230	4.3	0743	1.1	1502	4.2	2003	1.5
14 F	0307	4.1	0826	1.4	1546	3.9	2054	1.8
15 Sa	0356	3.8	0921	1.7	1644	3.7	2201	2.0
16 Su	0501	3.6	1034	1.9	1800	3.6	2324	2.0
17 M	0622	3.5	1157	1.8	1918	3.6	—	—
18 Tu	0042	1.8	0739	3.6	1306	1.6	2020	3.8
19 W	0142	1.5	0837	3.8	1358	1.3	2109	4.1
20 Th	0225	1.2	0923	4.1	1440	1.0	2148	4.4
21 F	0303	1.0	1002	4.4	1520	0.8	2226	4.6
22 Sa	0340	0.8	1040	4.6	1601	0.6	2303	4.7
23 Su	0418	0.6	1120	4.7	1644	0.5	2344	4.8
24 M	0501	0.5	1205	4.7	1725	0.5	—	—
25 Tu	0025	4.8	0543	0.4	1251	4.8	1807	0.5
26 W	0109	4.8	0626	0.4	1339	4.7	1848	0.6
27 Th	0154	4.7	0710	0.5	1429	4.6	1932	0.8
28 F	0241	4.5	0758	0.8	1522	4.4	2024	1.1
29 Sa	0334	4.2	0854	1.1	1624	4.2	2128	1.4
30 Su	0440	4.0	1005	1.3	1738	4.0	2249	1.6

Datum of predictions 2.7 m. below Ordnance Datum (Newlyn) or approx L.A.T. For H.W. at Dover (approx.) subtract 20 min.

Tide tables give height and time at major ports.

seen that the tidal curve is like a sine curve.

The amount which the tide rises and falls is not only important to know from the point of view of not running aground; it also matters when it comes to anchoring. Commonsense should dictate that you do not anchor where there is an obstruction shown on the chart, such as a wreck or rocks just below the surface. However, not all wrecks are shown on charts and you should therefore ask the local harbormaster, coastguard or anyone from the local sailing fraternity.

If you are anchoring offshore it may well be that the water *seems* deep enough and rocks shown on the chart are apparently well below the surface. But if you do not know the tide range and have, for example, anchored at high tide without bothering to make any calculations, you could end up aground or even stove-in when the tide falls. Equally, if anchoring at low tide, you need to know how much the water is going to rise so that sufficient line is allowed and you do not suffer the ignominy of being pulled under by your own too-short anchor line.

It is, of course, simple enough to discover the depth of the water at the point and time at which you anchor by using a leadline – a weighted rope with various depths marked off, often in meters nowadays. Having checked the depth you must then set it against the time, the state of the tide (whether it is ebbing or flowing) and tide tables, which will give you the time of high and low water and depths at each. From this you can work out your own 'rule of twelfths' table from which it will be possible to see exactly how much water there will be beneath the keel at any given time. Always remember, though, to add a safety margin to allow for movement of the boat by the waves or the wakes of passing craft. In addition, take into account the draft of your boat – the depth from the waterline to the keel. (On small boats this will be in centimeters or inches but on larger boats it will be a meter and more.)

When anchoring you should normally allow the line to be at least three times the depth of the water. However, do not be caught out here: if you are anchoring just before low tide in, say, half-a-meter of water, you could be in trouble if you intend to stay for several hours: the depth at high tide is almost certainly going to be more than 1.5 meters (ie, three times 0.5m). So, the length of the line should be three times the maximum depth expected during the time you are anchored or, safer still – since you might be delayed – three times the depth at high tide. One other point: if your line is nylon you should allow at least five times the depth. An anchor chain ideally lies along the bottom so that any pull on it helps to dig the anchor in; nylon does not lie and to achieve a near-horizontal pull a greater length is required.

When dropping anchor it is as well to remember

There are various methods of calculating the tides. One is based on the 'rule of twelfths.' As we have seen, the rate of rise and fall of the tide varies and is greatest at half tide. In the first hour after high tide the water falls one-twelfth of its total fall, in the second hour it falls two-twelfths and in the third, three-twelfths, by which time it is at half tide. Now the rate of fall begins to slow, but only gradually. In the next hour (the fourth since the tide turned) it falls three-twelfths again, in the fifth, two-twelfths and in the sixth, one-twelfth. The rate of rise follows exactly the same 'rule' as the tide comes in.

Thus, if the times of high tide and low tide are known and also the heights at each time, it is possible to work out the range and the height at any one time: divide the range by 12 and the time between two slack waters (turns of the tide) by six. If this is drawn as a graph with the base lines in hours and the vertical as the range, it will be

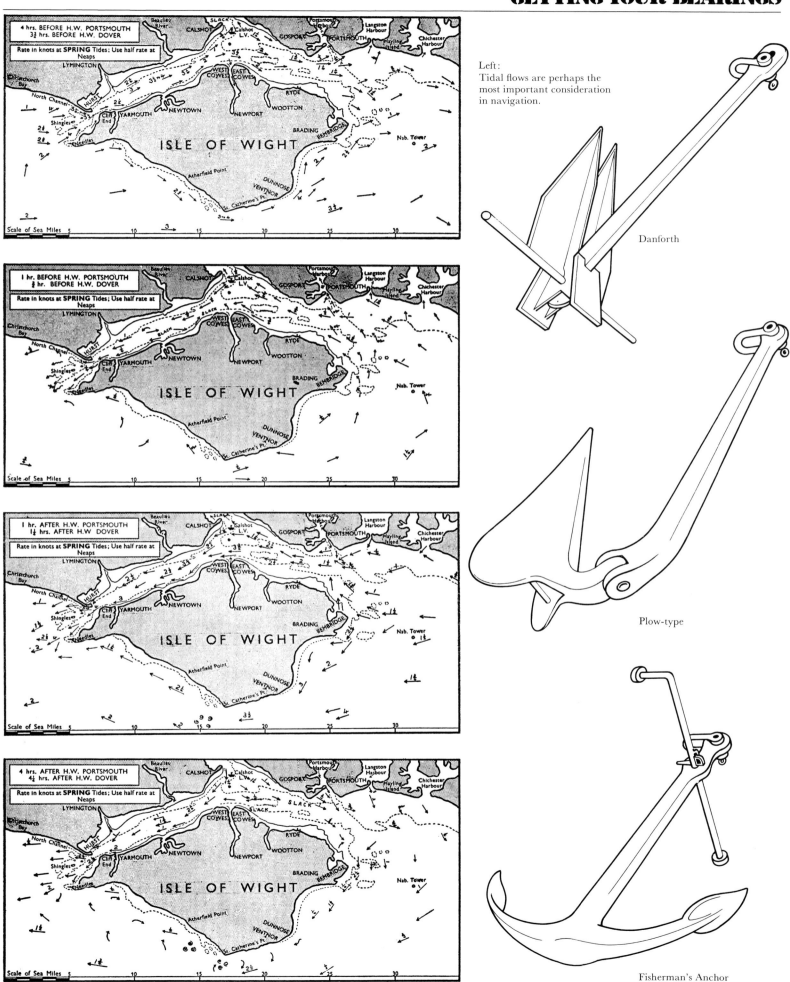

4 hrs. BEFORE H.W. PORTSMOUTH
3¾ hrs. BEFORE H.W. DOVER

Rate in knots at **SPRING** Tides; Use half rate at **Neaps**

ISLE OF WIGHT

Scale of Sea Miles

1 hr. BEFORE H.W. PORTSMOUTH
¾ hr. BEFORE H.W. DOVER

Rate in knots at **SPRING** Tides; Use half rate at Neaps

ISLE OF WIGHT

Scale of Sea Miles

1 hr. AFTER H.W. PORTSMOUTH
1¼ hrs. AFTER H.W. DOVER

Rate in knots at **SPRING** Tides; Use half rate at Neaps

ISLE OF WIGHT

Scale of Sea Miles

4 hrs. AFTER H.W. PORTSMOUTH
4¼ hrs. AFTER H.W. DOVER

Rate in knots at **SPRING** Tides; Use half rate at Neaps

ISLE OF WIGHT

Scale of Sea Miles

Crown Copyright

Left:
Tidal flows are perhaps the most important consideration in navigation.

Danforth

Plow-type

Fisherman's Anchor

137

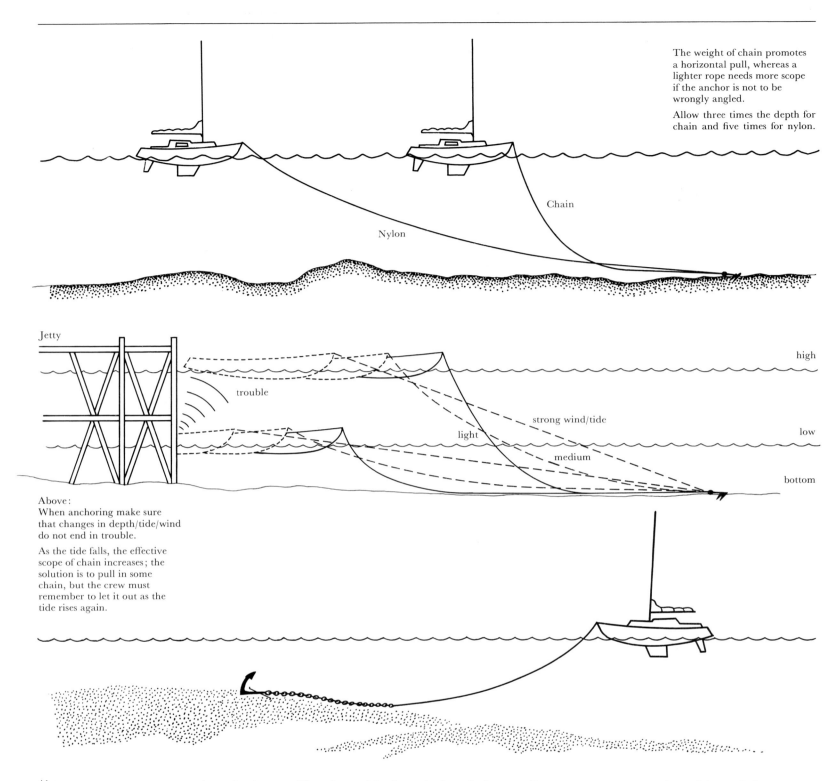

The weight of chain promotes a horizontal pull, whereas a lighter rope needs more scope if the anchor is not to be wrongly angled.

Allow three times the depth for chain and five times for nylon.

Chain

Nylon

Jetty

high

trouble

strong wind/tide

light

low

medium

bottom

Above:
When anchoring make sure that changes in depth/tide/wind do not end in trouble.

As the tide falls, the effective scope of chain increases; the solution is to pull in some chain, but the crew must remember to let it out as the tide rises again.

Above:
A length of chain between the mooring warp and the anchor helps to keep the pull on the anchor horizontal. The scope of cable veered should be at least five times the depth of water at high tide.

If an anchor rope is used, the anchor should have at least five meters of chain to help it bite and prevent chafe.

that the boat will swing with the wind and the tide as they change and that the radius of the circle it will describe will increase with the strength of both. This should be kept in mind in relation to any nearby surface obstructions such as other craft, jetties, mooring buoys and so on. They may seem to be a safe distance away when you anchor but if tide and wind are strong your boat is not going to ride gently almost above the anchor; it will pull out on the line and may hit one of those obstructions. Remember, too, that if you anchor at high tide, as the depth decreases there will be more 'free' line and the boat will swing in a wider arc the lower the water falls.

Let us now return to the subject of charts.

To determine his position on the vastness of the globe man devised the idea of dividing it into imaginary sections by drawing parallel lines around it 'horizontally' from the equator to the north and south poles. The position of a point or object in relation to the *parallels* is given as *longitude*. Imaginary lines were also drawn on the globe at right angles to the equator and running between the two poles, at which they converge; these are the *meridians* and the position of a point in relation to them is given as its *latitude*. The latitude 0° is the equator while the north pole is 90°N and the south pole 90°S. The meridian 0°

passes through Greenwich, England and since the globe is divided into 360° in this direction, longitude is calculated by 180° east and 180° west from Greenwich. Obviously, because they all meet at the poles, the meridians are not parallel to each other.

Until the middle of the 16th century charts were notoriously inaccurate because they had been drawn on the supposition that the earth was an extended plane. However, in about 1556 Gerard Mercator introduced his system of charts and today Mercator's Projection is the principle upon which charts are normally drawn. It is a projection of the earth's surface in the plane with all the meridians made parallel with each other.

To reproduce the globe's convex surface on flat paper involves distortion either of distances or of angles. So far as navigation is concerned, angles are of vital importance whereas distance is not as crucial. Mercator's principle therefore reproduces angles exactly but the distances are only accurate precisely on the equator, where there is no distortion since the meridians meet it, in fact and on the charts, at right angles.

As a result of this distortion, a straight line drawn between two points which lie on the same parallel on a chart does not represent the shortest distance between those points. This is because the chart is representing on the flat the real curvature

of the earth's surface. The true distance between the two points is therefore found by transferring that shape, known as the *arc of the great circle* to the chart. The great circle's arc is the same as that of a circle with its center the same as the center of the earth. On a short course the difference between the chart distance (known as the *rhumb line* course) and the actual distance (the *great circle* or *orthodromic* course) is so minute as not to matter.

The first sight of a chart can be a confusing experience for it seems to be covered with a mass of figures and symbols. In fact, the reading of a chart accurately requires a good deal of practice. Even when experience has been gained, it is never good enough to take a quick glance at the chart; always check and re-check your reading.

Having obtained the right chart for your particular needs you must do more than simply

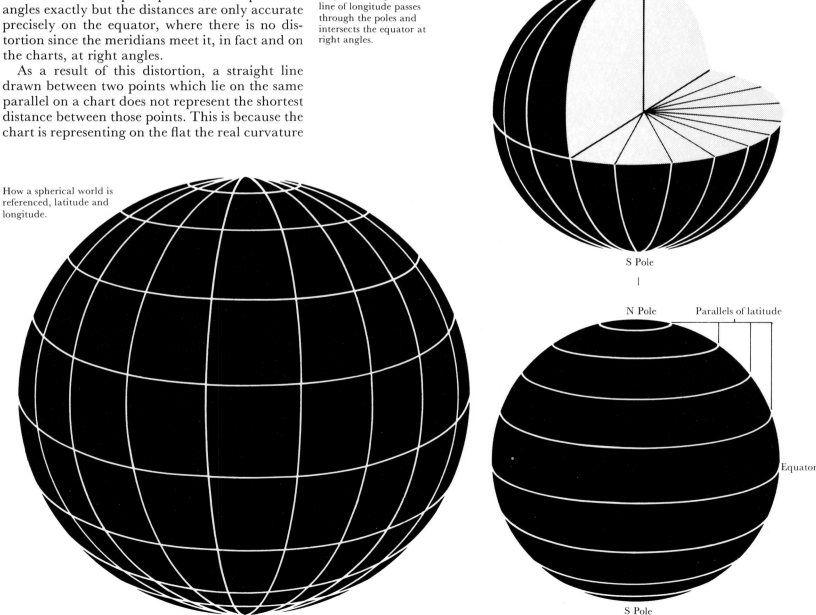

How a spherical world is referenced, latitude and longitude.

Degrees of longitude. Each line of longitude passes through the poles and intersects the equator at right angles.

N Pole

S Pole

N Pole   Parallels of latitude

Equator

S Pole

check that its title covers the correct area. Beneath the bold title there is a considerable amount of information which is important and should be read. For example, does the chart give depths in fathoms or in meters? (The newer charts have replaced fathoms with meters.) When was the chart compiled and up to what date have additions and corrections been made? (There may have been some important and recent changes such as new wrecks, shifting sand banks, added or changed markers and so on.) What is the scale of the chart and what are the datum levels?

All this information is included beneath the title, together with 'cautionary notes' which normally draw attention to things which may not have been included on that chart because its scale is too small. These may be wrecks, inner lights and buoys, radio navigational aids and the like. Additional cautionary notes may involve warnings about naval exercise areas, gunnery ranges, undersea cables and oil rigs. On smaller scale charts the navigator will normally be advised that details which have been omitted can be found on large scale charts for the area.

The chart will normally also carry at least one compass rose. This is a large double circle marked inside the larger circle with the degrees from true north (0°) clockwise round to 350° and 0° again. Extending from the center to just inside the large,

true north circle is an arrow which will be pointing slightly to the left of 0°. This indicates magnetic north and the line of the arrow runs through the 0° mark on the inner circle. Since magnetic north varies constantly, though only slightly, the inner circle will be printed with it set at the variation from true north for the year of publication and with a note stating what that was and the added point that it was decreasing at approximately five seconds annually.

Apart from this change in the variation year by year, any other changes or corrections since the chart was printed will be found in the *Notices to Mariners* which are published by the Hydrographic Department weekly and then as an annual summary. They are also broadcast as 'Urgent Notices to Mariners' after the weather forecasts from coastal stations where lights are concerned and, in general, are published by yachting journals.

Corrections should always be noted and marked clearly on the chart and in the left hand bottom margin, where the correction number and its date should be entered. Use indelible ink since there is every possibility that the chart will get wet at some stage. When actually working on the chart – plotting a course – always use a medium soft pencil and do not press too hard. Erase the lines with a soft rubber.

The various marks which you will see on any chart in addition to the figures for depths and heights are all usually quite easy to identify; stones and shingle, sandbanks, mud, buoys, beacons, lighthouses and so on are obvious either because of the symbols used or because they are identifiable in words as well. Along the edges of the chart are the scale markings: at the top (north) and bottom (south) there is the longitude scale which relates to the Greenwich meridian and on left (west) and right (east) is the latitude scale which is there to measure distances as well as to provide the information to give your exact position. The minutes of latitude are subdivided into tenths (200 yards).

Land is shown as yellow bounded by a continuous black line or a yellow line if it is a metric chart. The foreshore, which is covered and uncovered by the rise and fall of the tide is shaded and the nature of the bottom is indicated (on metric charts it is colored green). The sea itself is shown as either white or blue. Just as with heights on a land map, the contours of the underwater depths are indicated by lines linking places of the same depth. Most symbols and markings are common to all charts but there are some variations. The conventional signs and abbreviations are to be found in Admiralty Chart No 5011 but if you come across a chart with markings unknown to you, always ask the supplier for the book of abbreviations for the particular set of charts you are using.

Variation 8°20'W (1974) decreasing about 5' annually

MAGNETIC

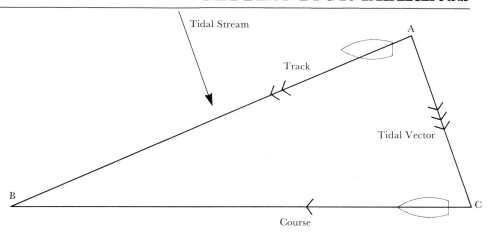

Tidal Stream

Track

A

Tidal Vector

B

C

Course

To make a track from A to B, the boat must head as though she were going from C to B to allow for tidal stream.

Plotting a course on a chart requires pencils, soft rubber, a pair of parallel rulers, a pair of dividers and, if the boat is large enough, a table on which the chart can be fully opened and laid flat. You cannot get away with the motoring navigator's trick of folding the map to just the section that you want.

For a comparatively short trip from one harbor to another it is best to plot your course from a point clear of the departure harbor to the clear water just outside the arrival harbor. Plotting your way out of the harbor and, for example, down to a river mouth, is not necessary since your course should be clearly defined on the chart itself and by markers along the channel. Having selected your departure and arrival points – and for the purposes of this explanation we are assuming that they are in a straight line – the parallel ruler is brought into use.

Lay the ruler on the chart and draw a line from departure to arrival point. Now make use of the 'crabbing' movement provided by the hinging of the ruler and 'crab' it across in steps to the center of the compass rose, making sure that you do not deviate from the parallel with your course line. The ruler will now be lying over the magnetic (inner) circle of the rose and from it you can read off the magnetic course.

Go back to the line you have drawn and work your way along it to make sure that it is not running across any dangerous points such as shallows, slightly submerged rocks or drying points – areas which will be above the waterline when the tide is low. If there are any hazards you must alter course well before them to make a dogleg round them and return to the original course.

That done you have before you on the chart your *theoretical* course. However, you must now take account of the effect which the tidal stream will have on your boat. The chart will carry a table which gives details of the speed and direction of the tidal stream in relation to a fixed point indicated on the chart and correlated by the six hours before and six hours after high water at the nearest port. Reference to the tide table for that port will give you the time of high water and the height – which will also indicate whether the tide is neap or spring. Reference back to the chart table will enable you to read off the speed in knots and the direction as a true bearing, *not* magnetic. From this, even though you may not be sailing near the fixed point on the chart to which the readings refer specifically, it is possible to assess with a fair degree of accuracy what effect the tide is likely to have on the boat. It may, for example, run particularly strongly around a promontory and cut across your course from starboard, tending to push you several degrees off course or, on the ebb, it may quite gently draw

you towards a sandbank which is marked by a buoy on the chart.

Since we have been able to discover the speed and direction in which the tide is likely to carry us we can also work out how far off course it may take us. To counteract that deviation the simple answer is to 'aim' that same distance in the opposite direction: if you are going to be taken x degrees west which will carry you y miles off course, you head x degrees east to cancel out the y miles.

The actual course you sail will, of course, also be influenced by the amount of leeway the boat makes because of the effects of the wind. Since the wind is not constant it is not possible to calculate what that leeway will be for it will vary from moment to moment and will be greater on one tack than on another. The answer, therefore, is to make periodic checks on your course by using the hand compass to discover how far from your intended bearing you may have strayed. After each check adjust your actual course to make up for the leeway.

When you are sailing or cruising close to the shore, landmarks can be used to check your course

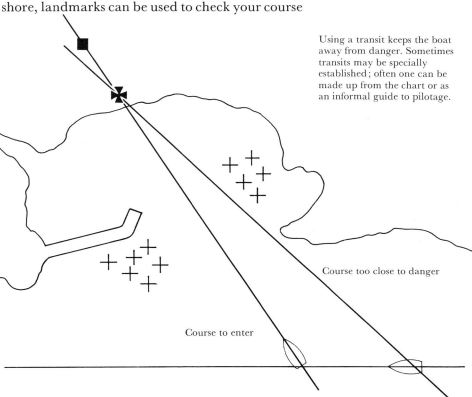

Using a transit keeps the boat away from danger. Sometimes transits may be specially established; often one can be made up from the chart or as an informal guide to pilotage.

Course too close to danger

Course to enter

without needing to use a compass because they are close enough to be exactly pinpointed. However, the further offshore you sail the less reliance should be placed on using the naked eye. It is far wiser to be sure by using a compass to take exact bearings than to make an approximation with the eye; an error of a few degrees can lead you into trouble or well astray.

Ideally, when sailing offshore but in sight of land you should select easily identifiable landmarks or 'transits' which are shown on the chart and visible from the deck. Using these you can pinpoint your position exactly and know precisely what lies below the surface ahead and around you. On a course which takes you some distance from but keeps you within sight of land, select a series of marks and sail by one after another. Once the mark can be positively identified you sail to keep it on a steady bearing. The bearing is layed off on the chart, back from the mark to the boat and this enables you to check where you are on the chart and whether there are any dangers ahead. Rather than simply standing on deck and pointing the compass at the mark it is best to use a fixed point on the boat – a shroud, for example – as a 'sighting line,' keeping the mark in line with it and checking your bearing from there.

However, beware that you do not pick the wrong sort of mark. A moored boat or a buoy do not make good marks because they both move with the tide and the wind sufficiently to throw your bearing out. Large fixed objects such as lighthouses, church towers or chimneys are ideal, groups of rocks less so because they are not always easy to pick out, single rocks even less because they can disappear completely (think of the state of the tide). Hills can be surprisingly deceptive if they have nothing atop them such as a distinctive clump of trees: they change completely in profile and 'character' as your own position changes and a hill which at first looked rounded may look entirely different from another angle.

Laying off a bearing can be used just as effectively with a mark away from which you are sailing as it can for one you are approaching. So long as you keep the mark behind you on the same bearing, checking with the hand compass, you can be sure you are on the right course and can make for your next mark.

Incidentally, if you are using this method you do need to know what to do if you find that the mark has drifted off a few points, ie, your course has altered a few degrees. If the mark is ahead and you find that it has drifted or 'drawn' to port (left) a little, the course must be altered to bring the bows those few degrees back to port (tiller to starboard). If the mark is astern and the mark draws to the left this will now be starboard (you're looking back) and it will, of course, mean that the bows have drifted to starboard and again must

be brought back a few points to port. That may sound like commonsense and indeed it is, but it is by no means unknown for a person taking a bearing astern to forget that he is looking away from the bows and to turn his instructions to the helmsman back to front.

Navigation can be made to sound extra-

The Sloop *Skibbereen* cruises slowly along the South Devon coastline towards Salcombe.

ordinarily complicated and certainly for those contemplating trans-oceanic voyages there is much more to it than we have stated here. Nevertheless, all is based on commonsense and a sound knowledge of how to read a chart and take a bearing, both of which are gained from experience. Ideally the learner should start off with a short, straight course and then gradually increase the length and complexity of the voyages.

Even the most experienced sailors are aware that the best made plans can be reduced to nought by the unexpected. A good sailor must be prepared to alter and revise his courses regularly and often instantly.

Visibility poor, perhaps 1½ miles. Slight haze, air moist indicating depression approaching with changeable windy weather.

10 WEATHER

Crewman hoists spinnaker halyard on Australian yacht *Ballyhoo* in ideal sailing conditions.

The one thing that no sailor can ever afford to do is ignore the weather – not just the weather at the time but, more important still, what it is going to be like later. And it cannot be over-emphasized that a feel of the wind, a look at the sky and a licked finger held aloft are no substitute for weather reports and forecasts by experts.

In fact, even before a voyage begins a sailor must take account of the weather and decide whether or not he should put to sea. There is a great temptation, particularly among keen sailors faced with a day which has not yet made up its mind, to trust to luck and the judgment of the local fisherman. The old chap might be full of wisdom and the lore of the sea and he may well come up with a colorful local rhyme: 'When tide be high and wind be west, to stay at home will suit you best,' or some such. This 'forecast' is likely to be about as accurate as crossing one's fingers and making a wish!

There are some weather indications which can immediately tell a sailor that he is not putting to sea today, or not yet. The most obvious is fog, which is one of the most frightening of all conditions to experience when actually at sea. Small boats caught in unexpected fog often have to be towed to safety by larger vessels equipped with radar and radio.

It is, of course, there – in that radio - that the sailor's great help lies: the regular shipping and weather forecasts broadcast by state-wide radio and television stations in the United States and by the British Broadcasting Corporation in Britain. The information is supplied by the National Weather Service in the United States and by the Meteorological Office in Britain. From a sailor's point of view it is the shipping forecast which is the most important since it is more precise than the weather forecast and deals specifically with conditions obtaining and forecast in defined areas. To the uninitiated they may be meaningless and sound like a string of strange-sounding names of places we have all heard of but could not find on a map. What, then, is the information given in these forecasts?

In the United States forecasts for those who are pursuing leisure sailing or cruising are the province of the US Government's National Weather Service, which is broken down into regional forecasting areas. The sheer size of the United States and the length of its seaboards make it impossible to broadcast one 'Shipping Forecast' covering all the sea areas.

Instead, hourly forecasts are broadcast by local television and radio stations, providing a general weather picture for metropolitan areas and supplemented by additional forecasts of sea and wind conditions in areas adjacent to popular sailing waters. In addition, it is possible to telephone for

Bottom:
Operating a Radio Direction Finder – a good means of fixing position when nothing is visible.

Opposite:
Fog is the sailor's worst enemy; radar reflector and sharp ears are the only protection.

forecasts which are updated hourly.

The National Weather Service does not use special sea area names such as the British 'Viking, Forties, Cromarty' and so on, listed later in this chapter. Instead, forecasts refer to waters by the name of the major bay, rivermouth or port in the area, such as Chesapeake Bay, Delaware Bay, New York Harbor, Tampa Bay, Key West, Pamlico Sound, Cape Blanco, Point St George, Point Conception and so on.

Wind warnings are broadcast whenever necessary. (In the same way the British Meteorological Office puts out immediate gale warnings to shipping.) They are repeated in the regular scheduled forecasts. On some Pacific Islands which are US possessions the US Navy's Forecasting Office issues forecasts for leisure sailing but in general these are not available to the public on the mainland.

Stations in North and Central America which transmit weather information for shipping on the high seas, in addition to forecasts for local waters, include Halifax, Boston, Annapolis, Portsmouth, Norfolk, Bermuda, Key West, Willemstad, Fort-de-France, Grenada, Destrellan, Barbados, Bridgetown, Port of Spain, North Post, Fort Collins, San Francisco and Vancouver.

Local water forecasts also come from Churchill, Coral Harbor, Frobisher Bay, Killnek, Inoucd-jouac, Poste de le Baleine, Goose, Carwright, St Anthony, Comfort Cove, Fox River, Mont Joli, Rivière du Loup, Grindstone, Stephenville, St Johns, St Lawrence, Charlottetown, Quebec, Sydney, Saint Pierre, Cansa, Montreal, Saint John, Yarmouth, Thunder Bay, Rogers City, Wiarton, Cardinal, Kingston, Toronto, Sarnia, Buffalo, Lorain, Marblehead, Port Burwell, Milwaukee, Port Washington, Sault Ste Marie, Duluth, New York, Ocean Gate, Amagansett, Baltimore, Cape May, Fort Macon, Charleston, Mayport, Jacksonville, Miami, Ojus, Nassau, Tampa, Saint Petersburg, Mobile, New Orleans, Grand Isle, Galveston, Port Aransas, Corpus Christi, Port Isabel, Ixtopalapa, Tacubaye, Islas del Cisne, Habane, Kingston, San Juan, St Kitts, Poine de Pitre, Dominica, St Lucia, St Vincent, Belize, San Pedro, Long Beach, Los Angeles, Eureka, Coos Bay, Astoria, Port Angeles, Seattle, Victoria, Tofino, Alert Bay, Spring Island, Bull Harbor, Comox, Sandspit, Prince Rupert, Annette, Ketchikan, Biorka, Juneau, Yakutat, Ocean Cape, Kodiak, Cold Bay, Cape Sarichef, Adak, Attea, King Salmon, Nome, Point Barrow, Inuvik, Coppermine and Cambridge Bay.

In Canada the Atmospheric Environment Service covers a large number of weather forecast areas from the Arctic to the west and east coasts. The Western and Central Arctic forecast areas are: North Alaskan Coast, MacKenzie, Amundsen, Dolphin, Coronation, Prince of Wales Strait, McLure, Melville, Queens Channel, Norwegian Bay, Eureka Sound, Robeson Channel, Kane, Northern Baffin Bay, Jones, Resolute Bay, Barrow, Lancaster, McClintock, Maud, Regent-Boothia and Southern Baffin Bay.

The Northeastern Coast areas are Churchill, Keewatin Coast, Central, Coats, Belcher, Foxe Basin, Foxe Channel, Nottingham, Ungava, Resolution, Frobisher Bay, Cumberland Sound, Davis Strait, Brevoort, Northeast Labrador Sea, Northwest Labrador Sea, North Labrador Coast, South Labrador Sea and South Labrador Coast.

Eastern Coast areas are Lake Melville, Belle Island Bank, Belle Isle, Funk Island Bank, East Coast, Northern Grand Banks, Southeastern Grand Banks, Southwestern Grand Banks, South Coast, West Coast, Harrington, Cabot Straits, Gulf Magdalen, Banquereau Bank, Cape Breton, Eastern Shore, Sable Area, Southwestern Shore, Brown's Lahave, Lurcher, Bay of Fundy, Northumberland Strait, Chaleur Miscou, Anticosti, Estuary Area, Lower St Lawrence, Middle St Lawrence and Upper St Lawrence.

On the West Coast the areas are Dixon Entrance, West Coast Queen Charlotte Islands, Hecate Strait, Queen Charlotte Sound, West Coast Vancouver Island, Juan de Fuca, Strait of St George, Johnstone Straits, Queen Charlotte Straits.

It is always worth checking with the local National Weather Service or with local radio stations to find out the times of forecasts, the type and the frequencies covered. For example, the Key West, Florida station puts out forecasts for the Western North Atlantic west of 35°W, including the Caribbean Sea and Gulf of Mexico at 0030 and 1230 on 5 870kHz and 0630 and 1900 on 25 590kHz. Each report includes any warnings of gales, storms or hurricanes but the first two are with an analysis for the area covered and the second two include forecasts.

San Francisco puts out information for 'Area Alfa' (North Pacific, equator – 30°N and east of 140°W), 'Area Bravo' (North Pacific, north of 30°N and east of 160°E) and coastal waters of Point St George to Point Conception. At 0420, 1620 and 2300 the information covers gale, storm and hurricane warnings for 'Alfa' and 'Bravo' followed by a weather summary for the areas. At 2200 coastal water warnings and forecasts are given. These are on 436kHz, 8 713.5kHz, 12 695.5kHz, 17 184.8kHz and 22 515kHz and cover 24-hour periods.

However, additional weather information from San Francisco is also available for those same three areas and for offshore waters (20–250 miles offshore from Cape Flattery, Washington to Guadalupe Island) on 4 371kHz, 8 738.4kHz, 13 161.5kHz and 17 307.7kHz as primary wavebands or on 8 735.2kHz and 13 151kHz as

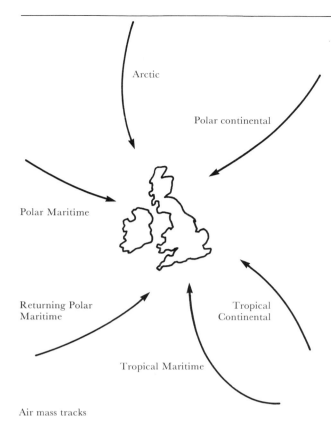

Arctic

Polar continental

Polar Maritime

Returning Polar
Maritime

Tropical
Continental

Tropical Maritime

Air mass tracks

Apart from telling the experienced listener that the low-pressure area is not very low at 1007 millibars (29.70in) but it is deepening, and that the high at 1022 millibars (30.14in) is going to be around that area for a time, the forecaster will give some other clues to weather without needing to explain them. A high high-pressure area adjacent to a low low-pressure is an indication that the weather is going to be tough going since the interaction between the two areas will create strong winds.

The forecaster will then give the Area Forecasts in detail, listing together those areas which will be having the same weather and working clockwise round the country from Viking round to Fair Isle, Faeroes and Southeast Iceland. For example, you may hear 'Viking, Forties, Cromarty, Forth, northeast 2 becoming north 3 to 4; rain; moderate becoming poor. Tyne, Dogger, variable 2 to 3 becoming north 3 to 4; fair; good becoming moderate, locally poor.'

What he has provided are the areas, the direction of the wind (remember, that the winds are

Fair weather sailing on the Hudson.

secondaries. This is broadcast at 0000, 0600 and 1500 and includes a summary, gale, storm or hurricane warnings and forecasts for the area affected.

There are at least a further 15 frequencies on which further weather information from San Francisco is broadcast, covering summaries, forecasts and warnings. On some frequencies warnings are broadcast immediately they are received and then repeated at fixed intervals, such as on the odd hour (0100, 0300 etc), while on others the warnings come only at fixed times.

From Buffalo, New York, sailing enthusiasts can receive an extremely comprehensive weather picture for Lakes Huron, Erie and Ontario and the St Lawrence River above St Regis on some eight frequencies throughout the day. Again, on some frequencies warnings are only given on receipt between 0930 and 0530, on others on receipt and on even hours plus 55 minutes thereafter (ie 0255, 0455 etc).

In the BBC's forecasts there is first the 'General synopsis' which gives a description of the prevailing weather conditions at a given time in given areas. It will indicate the positions of high and low pressure areas, their intensities and the directions in which they are moving. The figures which are given indicate the barometric pressures or intensities in millibars, in other words how high or how deep those high and low pressure areas are. Thus, the forecaster may announce 'Low, northwest Finisterre, 1007, moving northeast and deepening' or 'High, Biscay, 1022, slow-moving.'

In Britain millibars are used instead of inches of mercury. One inch of mercury equals 33.9 millibars; 1000 millibars equals 29.53 inches.

named with the direction from which they blow), its strength and forecast change of direction and strength, the general weather conditions and finally the visibility.

There is a set order in which the areas are listed both on printed forecast sheets and in broadcast announcements. That order is Viking, Forties, Cromarty, Forth, Tyne, Dogger, Fisher, German Bight, Humber, Thames, Dover, Wight, Portland, Plymouth, Biscay, Finisterre, Sole, Lundy, Fastnet, Irish Sea, Shannon, Rockall, Malin, Hebrides, Bailey, Fair Isle, Faeroes, Southeast Iceland.

The wind force given in the forecasts and in gale warnings is that of the Beaufort scale listed

earlier in this book. In miles per hour and kilometers per hour the scale translates as follows (Beaufort scale first): 1 – 2mph – 3kph; 2 – 5mph – 8kph; 3 – 9mph – 14kph; 4 – 13mph – 21kph; 5 – 18mph – 29kph; 6 – 24mph – 38.5kph; 7 – 30mph – 48kph; 8 – 37mph – 59.5kph; 9 – 44mph – 71kph; 10 – 52mph – 83.5kph; 11 – 60mph – 96.5kph; 12 – 68mph – 109kph.

Many listeners to the shipping forecast may wonder how sailors manage to keep up with the announcer. In fact nowadays they very often do not! Instead, they use a tape recorder. Also, for the sort of sailor about whom we are thinking – as opposed to the radio operator aboard a merchant

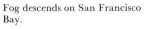
Fog descends on San Francisco Bay.

vessel for example – it is really only necessary to take account of the forecasts for the areas in which you are sailing and those adjacent. However, most chandlers do stock weather forecast maps and pads on which the areas we have listed are defined. The pads list the sea areas and provide space for the date and time of forecast and a column into which details of the forecast can be noted.

The maps also pinpoint and list coastal stations and these are included on the note pads as well. British coastal stations starting from the Fair Isle area are Sule Skerry (SS), Bell Rock (B), Dowsing (D), Galloper (G), Varne (V), Royal Sovereign

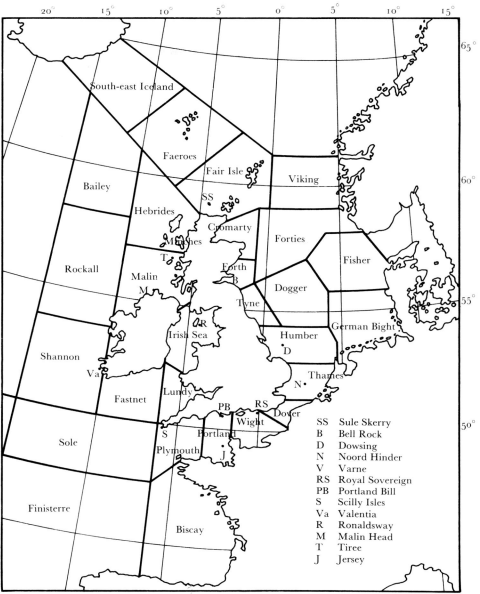

SS	Sule Skerry
B	Bell Rock
D	Dowsing
N	Noord Hinder
V	Varne
RS	Royal Sovereign
PB	Portland Bill
S	Scilly Isles
Va	Valentia
R	Ronaldsway
M	Malin Head
T	Tiree
J	Jersey

(RS), Portland Bill (PB), Scilly Isles (S), Valentia (Va), Ronaldsway (R), Malin Head (M), Tiree (T), and Jersey (J).

The final part of the shipping forecast is devoted to reports from these coastal stations and, again, it is important to know what the information is and in what order it comes. After the name of the station the forecaster will give the wind direction and force, the general weather situation, the visibility, the barometer readings and whether the barometer is rising, falling or stationary. Thus, he may be heard to say: 'Sule Skerry, north by east 3; rain; 6 miles; 1012 falling slowly.'

Assuming that you cannot do shorthand and do not possess a tape recorder, there is no need to panic about getting the information down; it is simply a matter of using annotation or devising your own form of 'shorthand.' For example, a forecast for Viking, Forties, Cromarty, Forth which said 'Variable 2, becoming south 3 to 4; fair; moderate, locally poor', could be noted down as V2 bec S 3/4 F M loc P.'

On the same basis, the report from the Sule

Frontal Development

Cold Front   Warm Front   Occluded Front

Isobars

High

Isobars

Low

Winds run parallel to isobars
in the Northern Hemisphere –
clockwise and tending outwards
around highs; counterclockwise
and inwards around lows.

at which the barometric pressures are the same. If the lines between the places with, for example, 1012, 1010, 1008 and 1006 (or 29.85in, 29.79in, 29.73in, 29.67in) are close together, the sides of the depression are steep and the stronger the winds will be. At the center of the contours there is the figure giving the lowest reading for that depression.

The high pressure areas do not follow quite the same general pattern of movement as the low in that they are more likely to move in from any point rather than usually from the west. It is this tendency for them to blunder in from anywhere that upsets the weather pattern – though anticyclones also tend to bring fine weather and to move quite slowly.

At the beginning of this chapter it was stated that a feel of the wind, a look at the sky and a licked finger held aloft are not a substitute for weather forecasts. That is true but with experience it *is* possible to gauge the weather prospects by looking for certain tell-tale signs in the sky which, in the Atlantic at least, are good indicators. In the Mediterranean the signs are not as reliable since this tends to be an area of less predictable weather and one in which the apparent pattern can suddenly be upset by unexpected local changes which have a 'ripple effect' on the general conditions.

The 'reading' of the sky is made possible by the fact that cloud formations do follow a certain pattern and build into a cloud system which gives a reasonable indication of the type of weather to come. Without going into a detailed description or analysis here, it can be said that a disturbance will send ahead of it cloud formations of a certain type and bring with it formations of a different kind. The area in front of the depression is the *head*, that within the depression is the *body* and that which follows is the *wake*. Further out from the depression there can be seen the clouds of the *cold edge* of the disturbance, or the *warm edge* or, at the outermost edge of a disturbance, where it meets the front of the next, the *boundary zone*.

It follows that if you can learn from experience the characteristic formations for each of these it becomes possible to tell whether a depression is on its way and to judge your own position in relation to it. Similarly it is possible to do the same for high pressure areas, though rather less reliance should be placed on these indications, which can change rapidly in some circumstances.

A point which should be remembered by those who may learn to 'read' the sky when sailing off Atlantic coasts, is that their experience will be of much less use to them in the Mediterranean. The weather in that area is a law unto itself, refusing to stick to the more-or-less well-defined patterns which are found in the Atlantic.

The difference is that the Mediterranean is an enclosed area whereas the Atlantic is open. In

Skerry station would be noted down as 'N × E 3 R 6mi 1012 ↓ S.'

By listening to the *whole* of the shipping forecast it is possible to get a good indication of the weather pattern over the whole of the British Isles and any movements of depressions which may affect the conditions in the area with which you are particularly concerned. Listeners will notice and television viewers will see that usually the UK receives its weather conditions from the west and that the pattern tends to be one of a series of depressions broken occasionally by 'highs.' The depressions normally bring with them wind and rain; a shallow depression means that the pressure will not be very deep and its 'sides' if they could be seen, would not be particularly steep but somewhat saucer-shaped. On a 'weather map' such as those shown in television forecasts the steepness of a depression – and of a 'high' or anticyclone, for that matter – is indicated by the spacing between the contour lines which are known as isobars. Just as a land map uses contour lines to join together places at the same height above sea level, so a weather map uses isobars to link places

Clouds forming overland may indicate local sea breezes but high cirrus indicates the approach of something more.

the Atlantic there is a far greater range of water temperature of 0° to 12°C, while in the Mediterranean the range is between around 10° and 16°C. This higher temperature in the Mediterranean means that the surface water is warmer than the lower layers of the atmosphere. These lower layers are warmed and become extremely humid and unstable. The pressure areas of the Atlantic are generally well-defined and the high and low areas cover vast areas. Over the Mediterranean they are far less well-defined and the centers of depressions and anticyclones are much smaller in area. There are, in fact, a greater number of conflicting 'lows' and 'highs.'

The foregoing, it must be admitted is a basic generalization of the differences, included only to indicate that the sailor should beware of using his Atlantic experience to try to gauge Mediterranean weather tendencies. To explain the differences fully would involve a complete book on meteorology.

Another generalization which is often made is that the barometer is the sailor's best friend. It is, so long as the sailor is *not* prepared to accept the evidence of his eyes in reading the barometer or barograph (which gives a continuous record of barometric readings) without checking.

The fact that the barometer reading has dropped a couple of millibars or fractions of inches since the last reading does not necessarily mean that a depression is on the way, any more than a rise of the same proportion means that an anticyclone is just over the horizon. What matters far more is the detection of any definite tendency on the part of the barometer, that is, changes in pressure upwards or downwards, over the course of a determined period, usually of three hours.

For example, if the barometer drops two or three millibars or several points of an inch over three hours it is a fair assumption that the weather is going to deteriorate somewhat, but not necessarily seriously; if the fall in the reading is as much as five or six mb or, say 0.17in, there is likely to be a strong disturbance on the way; more than that indicates that some extreme form of disturbance is around.

However, even observed tendencies in barometric readings cannot be regarded as absolutely sure signs of changes. There are occasions when a severe storm blows up despite the fact that the barometer has only indicated a tendency towards slightly worsening weather. This may be due to a purely local condition which has created a freak storm, the shallow depression having deepened suddenly; it may be simply because the barometer reading is often not exactly proportioned to the strength of the disturbance it is indicating (fortunately, the barometer tends more often to

'over-react' so that the storm turns out to be less severe than one might have expected).

With this proviso in mind, it is still right to pay due attention to what the indications are according to the barometer and to compare them with the indications of the sky itself. It is also dangerous to disregard the tendency shown by the barometer on the basis that 'the last time it did that, nothing happened.'

If the shipping forecast has predicted a gradual fall and instead, your barometer falls rapidly; if that fall is more than five mb in three hours and lower than that forecast – *then* you can expect severe weather.

Watch out, too, for the unexpected in thundery conditions, when the wind can increase suddenly from a gentle Force 1 or 2 to Force 6 or 7 (and more) without warning. In unstable conditions there is always the possibility that, having become used to a wind of Force 4 or 5, you are suddenly in a wind of Force 7. And if you have experienced a severe storm which then *seems* to have abated,

Fair weather cumulus.

remember that the 'eye of the storm' is not a figment of the fisherman's imagination.

Close to the center of a depression there will often be a settled area of comparative calm – the greater the violence of the storm the more marked is the calm. It does not, unfortunately always mean that the storm has passed; it may be that you are in the 'eye' and that the calm will be replaced by renewed rough weather quite soon.

A final point on the weather is that whenever a sailor is on shore in a strange port for a few days he would do well to listen to the forecasts and compare them with what actually happens. He may not become an expert on local weather conditions but he will at least pick up a few clues. Similarly, the novice can do no better than to gain experience by listening to the forecasts and noting how the weather really behaves in the period which the forecast covered. When he thinks he has gained sufficient knowledge to be able to make a forecast himself by 'reading' the signs, let him do so and record his own 'accuracy' rating!

Family cruiser fights a lonely battle to reach France in a mid-channel swell.

11 FOUL WEATHER

Admiral's Cup boats run in heavy weather in the Solent.

Although no small sailing boat should be out in really bad weather the likelihood is that every sailor will, sooner or later experience extreme weather conditions such as he never thought possible. Hopefully he will be on a boat which is large enough and have a crew experienced enough to handle the situation.

Bad weather, or heavy weather does not, in this context, mean just a rather messy day with strong winds and high seas. It refers to those conditions when the wind goes on increasing in strength until it is screaming through the rigging, bending every spar and making the deck tremble under its ferocious attack; it refers to the occasions when the waves mount higher and higher, their tops whipped into creaming foam which fills the air and lashes the face as the boat pitches and heels violently.

We have all seen photographs and films of such conditions and read descriptions of them yet, however expert the cameraman or however able the writer, no one can know what it is like without experiencing the moments when, despite everything else that may have gone before, you believe that *this* time the sea really has got you.

Apart from the danger which these conditions present in themselves there is the added problem of what they do to the people who are experiencing them. Whether sailing single-handed or with a crew, a sailor can suffer fright or sheer terror, a sapping not only of confidence but also of stamina, a feeling of total apathy and, of course, seasickness. Even without any of these effects, the strength of the storm can make every movement ten times more difficult and turn what would normally be a simple adjustment to gear or rigging into a mammoth task which leaves the sailor exhausted and bruised.

Fortunately, modern methods of boat building and the materials used, together with very strong fittings, mean that boats have a far better chance of surviving than they did a few years ago. Metal masts and spars, nylon sheets and gear made from very strong molded plastics or extremely tough metals mean that damage is greatly reduced – always assuming that all have been kept well maintained in the first place.

Before that moment arrives, when you find yourself in the middle of foul weather, you not only should know what precautions can be taken

Opposite:
A summer gale has dismasted this small sloop in the Solent; dismasting offshore is usually a more terrifying experience.

Bottom:
Life harnesses should fit tightly and have a positive locking system – they are only effective if clipped to a strong point on the deck, and should always be worn at night, in heavy weather, on watch alone and whenever you feel the need for added security in moving around the boat.

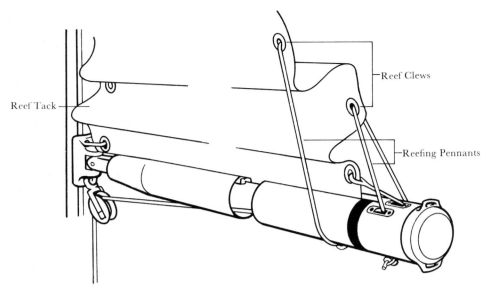

Reef Tack

Reef Clews

Reefing Pennants

A Modern Slab Reefing System

to help you survive the storm but also must know exactly where all the heavy-weather equipment is. This can include safety harnesses and lines, hanks, heavy weather sails, sea anchors and warps – heavy rope which can be trailed astern when running before the gale to help steady the boat.

Everyone on board should have worn and become used to his or her safety harness and should know that in storm conditions they must remain hooked to the safety lines at all times except when they are safely inside the cabin with the door shut. All equipment on deck such as spinnaker pole, oars, anchor, dinghy or life raft, should be securely lashed where they will not get in the way. In the cabin movable objects should be stowed away and clothing, blankets etc which need to be kept dry should be wrapped in plastic or waterproof bags before stowing. Once the storm breaks no one is likely either to want or be able to remain in the galley so it is wise for someone to take time to ensure that the crew will be able to grab at least a handful of biscuits when they have the chance, and also a hot drink, which can be prepared in advance and kept in thermoses. The pumps should have been checked regularly, not just to pump out the bilges but to make sure they are working properly. In the cabin checks should be made to ensure that as far as possible hatches, vents and doors are watertight. If the cabin has windows or large ports the builders may have provided safety panels and fixtures so that they can be screwed or bolted inside for protection if the glass breaks. If these have not been provided it is a simple enough job to make the panels yourself, ensuring that they are stored somewhere which is easily accessible and that screws or bolts are moused on; you do not want to be scrabbling around looking for them as the storm approaches.

It is highly unlikely that a storm will blow up so quickly that you are caught unawares. That only happens in films. Apart from the probability of a warning in the shipping forecast and indications from the behavior of the barometer, which we

have already mentioned, there will be physical signs of a deterioration of the general weather conditions, tell-tale warning cirrus clouds will be seen and there may well be a noticeable increase in the swell as well as in the strength of the wind well before the actual storm-force conditions arrive.

Since, therefore, you are likely to have some warning of the approach of foul weather there is a chance to prepare for action and even to take avoiding action. You are not going to know until it actually arrives whether the storm is going to bring conditions which are manageable, difficult to manage or absolutely unmanagable, in which event you can only do your best to hang on as the boat is tossed about.

It goes without saying that if you get warning of a storm and you are near any sort of harbor which you can identify both with the eye and on the chart, you make for it without delay. Even so, do not be in such a hurry that you forget to check your course and avoid any hidden dangers.

Even though a port is at hand it may not always be possible to reach its safety in time. If that is the case you must resist the very natural temptation to get as close to the harbor or to shore as possible. You may think that by doing so you are within easier reach of help; in fact you may well be placing yourself, your crew and your boat in greater danger, particularly if the gale is blowing towards the shore.

Not only is there the danger of being smashed onto shore or into harbor walls, there is also the increased danger presented by the fact that the sea will be far more broken and unpredictable in its behavior in shallower waters than in deep water. Always keep clear of shoals, rivermouths or narrow channels, where the conditions will be considerably worse and less predictable than in deep water, particularly if tide and wind are in opposition.

Having decided whether you are going to run for home or make for safer waters you should not make the mistake of sticking to that decision until it is too late to change your mind. One thing to bear in mind in a storm is that it will never behave predictably and you must always be prepared to change your tactics accordingly. Decisions must be taken and acted upon instantly.

Whether you decide to head for port or for open waters you will obviously either be running free (with the wind) or beating to windward. Whichever, the principles remain the same in a storm as in good weather but everything becomes more difficult and each reaction of the boat is exaggerated.

If your decision involves sailing with the wind free you will find that the boat becomes very unstable. She is presenting herself stern-first to the sea, making her extremely vulnerable and there

is an increased possibility that she will gybe or broach to, which in storm conditions can amount to disaster.

The safer course of action, if it is possible, is to bear to windward. One particular advantage is that, unlike running free, when any change in wind or general weather are less noticeable, a change in the wind is immediately detectable because the boat responds that much more quickly. Again, unlike sailing with the wind and presenting

a 'blunt end' to the sea, when beating to windward the boat will be using its strongest and most effective part, the bows.

That having been said, do not be misled into thinking that this course is going to be a comfortable one in such conditions. You will quickly discover that whereas in sailing free, the boat rolls heavily, in beating she will pitch violently and, even though you may try to luff into each wave and bear away slightly as you race down the other

A well-found yacht can stand any amount of pounding from the sea.

side, the boat will still slam with great force into the mounting waves.

As with sailing in normal conditions, so too with sailing in a storm: you must balance the amount of sail to the amount of wind. This may well involve reefing in to reduce the sail area evenly over all.

On modern boats the most common way of doing this on the mainsail nowadays is by roller-reefing. This involves rotating the boom about the gooseneck by using a handle that fits on to the reefing gear. The halyard is slackened off first and the handle turned to rotate the boom, thus rolling in the sail evenly along its foot. While this is being done the weight of the boom is borne by the topping lift and if the boom is lifted slightly by this it will help to make a neat job of the reefing. To accompany this method of roller-reefing it is usual for the kicking strap or vang to have a claw which fits round the boom and does not interfere with the rolling. If a claw is not fitted and the strap is attached direct to the boom it is necessary to remove it first. However, it is a good idea to fit it instead to a length of strong webbing which is

Ismana reaching under full main and working jib.

then attached to the strap fixture on the boom. The webbing can then be rolled into the sail as the reef is taken in, thereby enabling you to continue to use the kicking strap. Once the area of the sail has been reduced to your satisfaction the handle is removed and the halyard is tightened.

Another method of reducing the area of the mainsail is slab-reefing, which is used when the boat is not fitted with roller-reefing gear. This method involves the use of the short lengths of line known as reefing pendants or reef bands which hang in two or three rows above the boom from the luff to the leech of the sail below the small eyes. On the luff and the leech opposite each row are large eyes.

The principal here is that the halyard is slackened off and the sail lowered until one of the

rows of eyes and bands is just above the boom. Now the halyard is made fast again. The eye on the luff now becomes the new tack at the foot of the sail and is attached to the hook on the gooseneck (and lashed there if necessary in strong conditions). The other eye, on the leech, is now the new clew and is rove to the boom without pulling it too far aft. The reef pendants along the row are now knotted round the sagging portion of the sail so that it becomes neatly bunched.

When reefing, the whole length of the boom should be within reach so, ideally, you should be sailing to windward so that the sail is not full but also is not flapping. If needs be the boom can be held steady by the crew while the sail is reefed in.

The advantage of the roller-reef method is that you can adjust your sail area exactly to your own

requirements, while with slab-reefing you are limited by the spacing of the lines of reef points. However, roller-reefing is by no means infallible – the gear can jam – and it is useful to be able to revert to the hand-tying method.

Conditions which require you to reduce the area of the mainsail will also mean that you will possibly need to cut down the forward sail area by changing jibs. On a larger sailing boat there is always the likelihood that you will have a choice of jibs which can be changed to suit the conditions. Generally they are numbered according to size, starting from No 1 as the largest down to No 3 and then, smallest of all, the storm jib. This last is a very small sail which is rarely used except when heaving to.

Assuming conditions allow it, the best time to

A heavy weather start: you should leave enough time to check on optimum sail combination when you head for the start.

Gale-force winds demonstrate the power of the sea.

change jibs is when running free, keeping the wind slightly on the lee side of the mainsail, which is used to shield the jib so that it can be lowered without too much flapping. Always ensure before undoing the halyard that the replacement jib is in easy reach and that it has been packed correctly in its bag so that the tack can first be shackled to the stern and the rest of the sail then hanked on to the forestay. The sheets are next to be shackled into place and then the replacement jib is ready to be hauled up.

How many times in nautical tales on television or in the cinema have you heard the expression 'Heave-to!' yelled at the top of an actor's voice? It is the story-teller's favorite line for adding extra drama to a storm scene.

In fact, heaving-to *is* the classic way of riding a storm by 'sitting it out' until conditions improve. The method will vary according to the performing characteristics of individual boats almost as much as it does between different types of boat. Nevertheless, the basic principle is that the mainsail, well reefed, is sheeted home and the headsail is sheeted aback; the former will tend to make the boat luff up but the latter will make her bear away. The result should be that, if the two tendencies balance, the boat will lose virtually all her headway but will have a good deal of leeway. The leeway has a positive benefit because it causes a certain amount of turbulence in the water to the windward of the boat which, in breaking the form of the waves helps to reduce their size somewhat in the immediate vicinity.

By heaving-to you can wait out the storm, bow on to the wind and can even lash the tiller and leave it in some types of boat which achieve good balance.

Attaining the correct balance is a matter for experiment since one boat may heave-to happily with the mainsail reefed down as far as possible while another might require only a storm jib. While it is perfectly possible to lash the tiller (again, the position in which it is lashed for maximum balance is only found by experience) there is a proviso about leaving it and about going below for any time to dry out. Always check that there is plenty of room to leeward so that you can drift freely without hitting anything.

Earlier we mentioned sailing with the wind free; if conditions become so severe that you can no longer maintain your course and have, in effect, to turn tail and allow the wind and sea to carry you before them you are 'running before the storm.' This can be an extremely hazardous thing to do since you are virtually giving the boat over to the elements and all the difficulties of running free become accentuated. The boat will be even more unstable and it may be necessary to go under bare poles to reduce your speed. In addition, you may be in danger of being carried onto rocks or shore. Before deciding to run before the storm you should be sure that you are going to be carried in open water.

Whatever else you do, you should not be tempted into using a sea anchor when running before. Essentially, a sea anchor is a large canvas

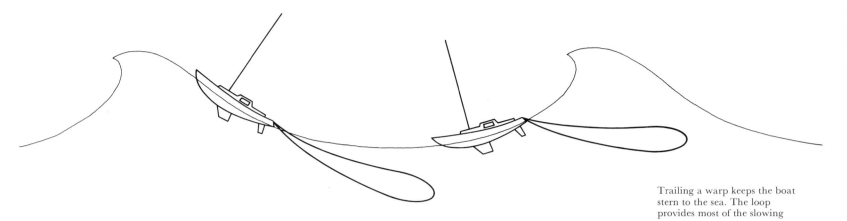

Trailing a warp keeps the boat stern to the sea. The loop provides most of the slowing power.

bag which is trailed in the water with its mouth held open by a metal ring so that it 'bites' the water to create considerable drag. The bag is weighted so that it sinks well below the surface but does not touch bottom and usually has a second line, a tripping line, attached to its closed end. This can be used for hauling in, so that the bag is turned about and emptied while still in the water, making the job of bringing it in considerably less of a strain. One of the problems of a sea anchor is that its braking effect can be so great that the boat actually makes sternway. In addition, it tends to drag the stern down.

A better way of reducing speed, particularly when running before, is to trail a heavy warp over the stern. The warp should be at least six meters long and should be attached by both ends at the bow and fed back over the stern, running back outside the shroud, through cleats at the aft and trailing as a loop in the water. This will considerably reduce your speed without dragging the stern down so drastically so that the waves do not come over the stern as often. However, you will find that you still have no control over your course when running before and if the storm continues to increase in force the warp should be brought in because, instead of helping, they become a positive danger in really severe conditions approaching hurricane force.

The last resort may be to anchor in the storm. This may sound a strange thing to do because you are making the boat a 'sitting target' for the wind and the sea. Indeed, that is what you are doing but that may well be better than being carried out to unknown waters or, worse still, being driven on shore. It is no earthly use simply deciding that you are going to drop anchor and casting one over the side. You must try, even in the midst of the storm, to select a spot which the chart shows has a good bottom on which to anchor. If you have – as you should have – several anchors aboard, use all of them, dropping them in line and using all the line immediately so that the anchors have the best chance of going straight to the bottom and biting at once; if they start to drag before they can bite there is a strong possibility that they will not hold you at all.

Calm after storm.

Heaving up sail on an old gaff cutter.

12 A 'NOBLE PRACTICAL ART'

'The noble practical art of rigging and working a ship and performing with effect all her various evolutions at sea.' That is how Admiral Smyth, to whom I have referred before, defined seamanship. Some of that art we have touched upon already and some we have considered in detail.

Of one thing you can be certain: without the ability to tie a good knot or make a good splice you will never be a good seaman. You will need to know which knot or splice it is best to use in a particular circumstance and when not to use a knot! For example, once you have hoisted the sails you will find that there is a good deal of halyard lying on the deck. The sail is made fast by cleating the halyard but what about the rest of the rope which, obviously, cannot be left there? The answer is simply to coil it neatly – and there is even an art in that. Take the end of the rope nearest the cleat in your left hand (if you are right-handed) and then wind on the remaining slack with your right hand, laying it across the left palm in a clockwise direction and making loops of about 18 inches (46cm) in diameter until you reach the end. Then bunch the coil together in the middle and wedge it between the halyard and the mast,

Coil hitch.

sliding it down to the top of the cleat. The coil is then held firm by the tension on the halyard yet is easily released in a hurry.

With thicker and longer ropes – mooring ropes, for example – make a larger coil on the deck and secure it by using a *coil hitch* before stowing it in the fo'c'sle or locker. The coil hitch, like many other seaman's knots, is based on a simple half-hitch: the free end of the rope is passed round the body of the coil in a figure-of-eight fashion (the first turn being the 'half-hitch'), the end is then tucked under the downward 'stroke' of the eight to hold it fast and the knot is worked tight.

Probably the best known knot of all is the *reef knot* – which is not, incidentally, used to tie reefs. Its usefulness at sea is very much a matter for argument: some swear by it for use as a simple knot on which a great deal of tension will not be put; others aver that it should not be used at sea because it either slips or jams tight. The choice is yours; you will only discover whether or not it is useful to you by trying it out, bearing in mind its limitations: it is not a heavy-duty knot, nor should it be used to tie together ropes of different thicknesses. It *is* useful, however, for keeping out of the way a coil of rope that cannot be stowed: use a couple of lengths of cord to lash the coil against the guard rails.

The *reef knot* is very simple to tie and just as simple to make a mess of and turn into a 'granny knot.' Take the two ends of the cord or rope and lay the left over the right; pass this left end behind the right and back to the front; now pass the right-hand end (yes, it is the one which was originally

Reef knot.

Sheet bend.

Cleating down halyard.

Bowline.

Changing headsails during
Ocean race.

in your left hand) over the left, behind it and back to the front. If the knot has been correctly tied it will consist of two loops which can be pushed apart, the ends of each passing through the bight (loop) of the other. It becomes a 'granny knot' if, as often happens, the end of rope you use to start the knot is not used throughout. Many people make the mistake of starting the 'over-and-under' with one end and completing with the other; the result is an untidy knot that slips.

The knot you should use to join two separate ends of rope is the *sheet bend* but you can only do this when neither rope is under tension. Make an open loop in your left hand, with the end of the piece of rope nearest you; bring the end of the other rope up through the loop and pass it behind the loop by taking it under the short end (first) and the long end; bring it back over the loop and pass it under itself (but *not* back into the loop again); pull tight. The two short ends should be on the same side of

the knot otherwise it is a left-handed sheet bend which is not quite so secure as the knot with the two short ends lying on the same side.

One of the most useful of all knots is the *bowline*, which can be tied in all kinds of rope, without either slipping or jamming, to provide a loop for numerous purposes such as round a bollard, putting an 'eye' on the end of a mooring line or attaching a rope to a ring or eye. The bowline is another knot which can only be made on slack rope but it is one which is of such use that you should learn to tie it in the dark.

Having decided how big you want the loop to be you make a small eye in the rope about twice the length of the loop from the end of the rope. The main length of rope (the standing part) lies behind the eye. The end of the rope is brought up through the eye, round the back of the standing part and back down into the eye. Work the knot tightly by holding the free end which has just been

Round turn and two half hitches.

passed through the eye and pulling on the standing part of the rope so that the eye closes to leave the loop. The only precautionary note here is to ensure that the eye is formed by laying the free end *over* the standing part of the rope; otherwise the whole thing collapses.

This knot is one which is used to make a loop which lies loose and the rope is therefore subject to chafe when it moves. A knot which is used for making a tighter fastening to avoid chafe is the *round turn and two half hitches* which can be used through a ring or on upright or horizontal spars etc. From the front the rope is passed through the ring, back and through again to make the round turn; the free end is then passed in front of the standing part, behind it and back *over* itself to make the first half hitch; then a secnd half hitch is made exactly the same way before the knot is pulled really taut. The great attraction of the round turn and two half hitches is its versatility since it can be used in place of the bowline or for all manner of 'tying-up' jobs involving fastening a rope to something more solid such as a bucket handle, rail, fender, ring or spar. It should not be used to fasten rope to rope. (For this purpose use the sheet bend already described.)

The *clove hitch* is a knot which can be quickly and easily made. It has excellent holding power yet can be eased off without untying and it can be tied under tension. The standing part of the rope is half-hitched around a bollard or post so that the free end (fall) of the rope is underneath; a second half-hitch is made by looping the fall over the bollard, again with the free end underneath so that it is 'sandwiched' between the two hitches.

Another version of this is the *tugman's hitch* which, as its name implies, is mainly used for tow ropes and can be tied while the rope is running. The free end of the rope is dropped round a bollard or samson post, over the top of the standing part. This immediately stops the rope running. Further turns round the post are made as necessary from the free end and the final turn is made as a bight by looping it, passing it under the standing part and dropping the loop over the post. Make sure that the free end is at the top of the loop so that it is 'bitten' by the standing part as the loop is dropped over the post. Ideally the free end should be turned round a cleat as a safeguard against slipping.

If a permanent or semi-permanent join between two ropes is required the *fisherman's knot* is ideal as it is extremely difficult to untie once it has been tightened. Lay the two pieces of rope to be joined end to end but with the ends overlapping by about one foot; loop one end under the other about six inches in from its end and bring it over the standing part and over itself, back behind itself and through the eye you have formed, passing it under the standing part and out of the eye. Do the same with the other piece of rope and then pull the two knots towards each other. In effect, you are simply tying two stop knots on the end of each piece of rope and allowing them to slide together.

There are, of course, many more knots which can be used – something like three thousand more – but with these eight you should be able to cope on board. However, if any rope is to retain its usefulness it must not be allowed to fray at the ends. Any rope which has been cut must be whipped at the end to prevent its separate strands coming apart. This applies as much to manmade fibers as to natural fibers: a nylon rope cut with a hot knife – as it should be – may look as though its ends have been sealed by the heat but the sealing is only temporary.

Always use a double thread or strong twine for whipping and a large needle (size 15 or 14, the latter being the larger). Pass the needle through the rope about one inch (2.5cm) from the end and draw the thread through. Wind the thread tightly round the rope, working towards the end and making sure that the strands lie flat. About a quarter-of-an-inch (6mm) from the end of the rope, push the needle through the rope and again pull the thread tight. Now make a 'seizing' by passing the needle under the whipping down to the starting point, running at a depth of about a third of the rope's thickness, pull tight and repeat twice more so that the strands of the whipping are pulled together. Do this again at two or three equally spaced points round the whipping and finish off each by half-hitching the thread round

Clove hitch.

Tugman's hitch.

the seizing; push the needle through the rope and cut the thread neatly close to the rope's surface.

An alternative method of whipping is to loop the thread along the rope for about one inch (2.5cm) parallel to the lay of the strands, the loop being towards the end of the rope. Leaving half-an-inch of the free end spare wind the thread over the loop and round the rope back towards the end. When only the tip of the loop is showing beyond the whipping, pass the thread through it and cut the thread. Now pull the free end of the thread at the starting point of the whipping so that the loop is dragged out of sight under the threads, drawing the end of the last turn with it. Cut off the free end of thread close to the first turn of the whipping.

The art of splicing a rope successfully – which implies tidily as well as strongly – is a different one and requires plenty of practice. There are numerous different kinds of splices for different purposes but the most useful to know is that for making a permanent eye round a grooved metal or plastic thimble.

If a conventional stranded-fiber rope (as opposed to a synthetic rope) is used, the strands are separated and a bight is made of the right size to fit snugly round the thimble. The standing part of the rope is held in the left hand and the bight made towards you with the right. The center one of the separated strands is the first to be tucked under a strand in the standing part and pulled tight to the required size of the eye. Follow with the next strand on the left, which is tucked under the next strand above on the standing part (ie again, the next on the left). Now turn the loop over and tuck in the third strand from right to left so that all three strands have been fed in against the lay of

the strands in the standing part. Continue tucking in the strands and pulling tight, always in the same order – from right to left - and working each tight. Four or five tucks should be sufficient. To finish the job neatly it can be whipped.

This method will not work with synthetic rope which is shiny and extremely stiff when new. Instead the rope should be held firmly round the eye with a free end which is about four times as long as the diameter of the rope. It is extremely difficult to pass a needle through the full diameter of the rope so use a size 15 needle to sew along either side of the rope with nylon thread, penetrating the rope at about a quarter of its width and drawing the thread through tightly. Though it is not entirely necessary the job is given added strength as well as greater neatness by using a whipping over the sewn section.

Fisherman's Bend.

Osmosis of a glass fiber hull is treated by stripping down affected layers of lamination before resurfacing.

13 LAYING UP

The bosun's chair makes possible a thorough inspection of halyard sheaves and other masthead fittings.

Top:
Fitting a wind indicator to the masthead.

Bottom:
Shoring up is best left to professionals but amateurs can produce good paint-work.

In a season's sailing a boat undergoes a considerable amount of wear and tear, not to say a fairly hefty pounding under some circumstances. It would be a lucky owner who goes through a year without having to replace some piece of gear, be it a halyard, a sail, a mast, rudder blade, tiller arm or one of any of the many smaller fittings. It may well be that the hull of the boat itself becomes damaged. Fortunately fiberglass boat hulls can be mended quickly and quite simply with one of the many quick-drying, hard-setting cement compounds. Stove-in timbers are another matter and require a higher degree of craftsmanship – and consequently of cost – to replace them.

So far as day-to-day or running maintenance is concerned, it should be based on the policy that you never leave your boat without checking that all is in order and you never set out without an even more thorough inspection. Nor should the boat be left for any length of time without someone taking a look and noting any signs of wear or corrosion.

The battle against corrosion, particularly if your sailing is done on salt water, is a ceaseless one and the need to inspect metal parts and articles for signs of it cannot be overstressed. A shackle pin which shears through at a crucial moment can lead to disaster. The greatest aid is a light greasing of metal parts and particularly of any which move or have movement through them. Similarly, the threads of all bottlescrews should be greased and checked for free turning.

Sails and sheets are obviously going to experience a great deal of chafing and an eye should be kept on this so that no sail or rope is allowed to chafe to a point at which it becomes unsafe. Sails made from synthetic materials are, in themselves, extremely strong but they do have a disadvantage in that any stitching on them will tend to stand proud and therefore be prone to chafe. Check regularly along seams and where any chafed stitches are found sew in some fresh stitches, allowing a good overlap on either side of the damaged point and ensuring that broken threads have their ends sewn in to prevent 'running.'

While they have the advantage of extra strength, ropes made from synthetic fibers have one particular disadvantage: they deteriorate when exposed to strong sunlight. When not in use they should, therefore, be stowed away. Similarly a synthetic sail should not be left exposed unnecessarily.

Throughout the season and particularly towards the end of it there will be a number of points which occur to you about the boat's maintenance that do not require immediate attention. If you decide that a job can wait until the boat is laid-up there is always the possibility that, when that time comes, you will forget all about it. It is a sensible tip to keep a notebook or job list and to jot down such jobs. Even having done that, never forget all about it: check the list every now and again, see what is on it and then make a point of inspecting fixtures and fittings mentioned to ensure that they have not deteriorated to the point that they cannot after all wait.

The part of the hull below the waterline is the area of a boat which is most likely to escape regular inspection if it is not, like a small sailboat, brought out of the water frequently. With a large boat an inspection can best be made by drifting it on to a cradle at high tide and waiting for the water to fall so that you can walk – or wade – round. An alternative is to have it lifted by crane, which is a complicated and costly business and one not to be undertaken without expert advice.

Top left and Top right:
Mast hoops, parrell beads,
bullseyes and bolt rope (right),
just part of the beautifully
restored rigging on an American
sail trainer in Milbay docks
prior to the start of the 1976
Tall Ships races to America.

Bottom:
Craning out requires some care.
This photograph shows the use
of wire slings. The other
method employs webbing
strops which should always
be used with adequate
spacing to ensure they do not
place compression loads on the
deck. Particular care should
be taken to ensure that they
do not rest over the propeller
shaft.

A small sailboat can quite happily spend the winter turned over on the ground once the mast has been unstepped and taken away for safe-keeping along with all other movable equipment. Ideally, since it is the cheapest and most secure way, it is taken home by trailer at the end of the season but if this is not possible, keep it somewhere that is at least relatively secure and has the benefit of some form of enclosure and regular visits.

If the boat, whatever its size, has woodwork on board or a wooden mast, any scratches should be given a fresh lick of varnish at once. All woodwork can be rubbed down and given a fresh coat during the winter.

Wooden-hulled boats require special attention. Like all boats their underwater parts should be treated with one of the many anti-fouling or inhibitor paints which prevent various marine growths from attaching to the bottom. This is particularly important for the wooden hull because the graining of the wood is an attraction to spores. The anti-fouling paints are made to a variety of formulas to suit different water conditions, so it is always advisable to check which sort is best for the area in which you will be sailing. The paint is effective in water but loses efficiency when it is left dry, so it is best to apply a fresh coat just before the start of the new season rather than in the early part of the 'closed season.'

If, when the wooden-hulled boat is first out of the water, it shows signs of heavy growths of marine vegetation it should be given a thorough scrubbing and allowed to dry out. The drying out

least a week to dry before the boat is re-launched.

Whatever type of hull your boat has, the inside needs just as much attention as the outside. Every part of the interior should be thoroughly cleaned out. Ideally, washing out should be done with really fresh water to avoid a lingering smell which, if the boat is left closed up through the winter, will leap out to greet you as you open her up for the next season. In particular, make sure the bilges are cleaned out and dry.

Even if fresh water is used, you will still be greeted by that smell if the inside of the boat is not ventilated thoroughly. This does not just mean that you should have vents from the open air to the cabin but also includes air holes in lockers, hatches and doors left open or ajar and cupboards

Top:
Blowlamps are the most effective way of stripping old paint but their use on some types of anti-fouling can produce dangerous toxic fumes.

Above:
A bright spring day makes preparation work for the summer more attractive.

Top right:
A plastic cover provides effective protection from the elements but it is important to allow reasonable circulation of air.

Right:
Boats laid up under cover on the Hamble river.

can be done in a cradle or on legs or it can be against a harbor wall if the spot where the boat will rest is carefully selected. Some harbors provide special 'drying-out posts' against which the boat can rest when the water recedes but many do not. In the latter event you should inspect the dry spots in the harbor which are beside a good wall and are flat. Here the boat can rest, balanced against the wall when the water recedes. However, you must select the right time to carry out the operation: when the range of the tide is sufficient to float the boat on, dry out and float off again.

As the tide recedes after the boat has been floated on, you will need to be well fendered along the side which will rest against the wall and you should make sure that the boat will tilt towards the wall when she grounds and is held securely against the awful tendency for it to fall over the other way! Remember, too, that the older the wood, the greater the attention needed and the more care in inspecting for signs of weakness. Apart from scrubbing down, the whole hull will require painting and the coats must be given at emptied and either left open or provided with some form of venting. The ideal way for most modern boats to winter is under cover but even then the need for thorough ventilation remains.

The likelihood is that if you can winter the boat under cover the mast will have to come down, along with the rigging. If the mast is taken out for the winter this can be done without removing all the rigging but you must ensure that it is laid flat and covered. If a wood mast is involved flatness is crucial and can only be achieved by laying it on the straight side – the one with the groove or track.

In the open, dis-masting will not be necessary unless you have an essential repair to carry out aloft. However, the fact that the mast and rigging remain up does not mean that they do not need

Waiting for the tide to ebb before a midsummer scrub-down.

Bottom left:
Chocking up on dry land allows easy access for keel and hull maintenance – the dangers of insecure chocking are obvious and it is not something the inexperienced should attempt.

attention. Wooden masts and spars will require varnishing, metal ones need light greasing and a greasy rag should be run over halyards and all other metal parts. Sheaves and blocks need oiling. Sails will require a good soaking in fresh water and thorough drying before being folded away.

If a boat is kept in a harbor which offers all-round shelter and is constantly supervised by a harbormaster or responsible person, it is safe enough to let the boat spend the winter in the water. In fact, older wooden boats actually benefit from remaining in the water as much as possible – though they will obviously require occasional inspection. This, however, does not apply to plywood hulls, which tend to absorb the water and deteriorate between the ply layers. Metal hulls will not normally suffer from remaining afloat but some care should be taken that galvanic action is not set up between two metal hulls lying side-by-side or between aluminum close to brass or copper fittings. There is, of course, also the possibility of two metal hulls damaging each other if they are moored side-by-side and continually bump together.

Fiberglass hulls require virtually no maintenance. They do not need to be painted and because of this they do tend to become stained and dulled after a time. However, most stains can be removed easily enough by a good scrubbing with plain seawater or fresh water. The sooner the scrubbing is done, the easier will it be to remove the stains. A complete scrub-down and rub-down will restore at least some of the gloss to the finish but a better result will be achieved by using a proprietary cleaning fluid, followed by a fiberglass polish. Though almost maintenance-free, this sort of hull still needs the coat of anti-fouling fluid to discourage the growth of marine life. Though barnacles and weeds do not attach themselves as easily to fiberglass as they do to wood, they will grow there given half a chance and their protruberances will have an effect on the boat's performance.

An important point about laying-up, wherever it may be done: always remove all perishable equipment and anything that may be a tempta-

tion to the light-fingered, such as compasses, charts, navigation tools, anchors, paddles and oars, etc. Take the opportunity, too, to clear out any old pieces of equipment which you know perfectly well you will never use again or which you have hung on to 'just in case. . . .' That includes that short length of rope you thought, three years ago, just might come in useful, the block that jammed every time you used it, the old chart case mended with tape and yellowed with age. It is not a problem in a small boat, of course, but the cabin of a yacht or cruiser can become almost like a garage or a garden shed for the number of odds and ends it collects in its dark corners and cupboards. If a gas container is used aboard, be certain that the gas cylinder is disconnected and taken away with you. It is never advisable to leave it aboard as it presents a potential hazard even though it may be perfectly sound and free from leaks when it is left. Similarly, disconnect all electrical equipment, remove batteries and store them at home, and clean all connections before lightly greasing them. Take the batteries out of flashlights and start the next season with a new set.

All safety equipment should be thoroughly checked – life rafts require an annual check by the agents – and life jackets, buoyancy aids and harnesses should be washed in fresh water and thoroughly dried.

Engine maintenance is 'a whole new ball game' which requires separate reading. Suffice to say that you should not attempt your own maintenance and repair work unless you really know what you are doing; you may think you are saving money but a job not properly done can prove costly in the long run – and you can be sure that the breakdown will occur at the worst possible moment! It is most important to drain off fuel, whether it be gasoline or diesel. The lubricating system of a diesel engine should be filled with a recommended inhibiting oil. The batteries and generators of gasoline or diesel engines should be removed and the engines cleaned on the outside with a de-greaser followed by a wipe with a lightly oiled rag. Drain the water from the cooling system. During laying-up, turn the engine over by hand occasionally to keep the pistons free.

Outboard motors are best left to the attentions of the nearest appointed agent for servicing. On no account should they be left on board either with or without fuel in the tank or with water trapped in the cooling system. Finally, remove all tools from the boat.

In addition to the checklist you have made during the season of jobs to be done, it is a good idea to make another list when laying-up. This one itemizes everything you have taken off the boat with a note beside those fittings which need replacing before the start of the next season.

A visit to a boat show is an enjoyable way of assessing the market.

14 BUYING A BOAT

Learning to sail in a Skipper sailboat.

Deciding what sort of boat you want to own and whether it should be new or second-hand depends so much on personal preference and the depth of one's pocket that it would be quite wrong to attempt, in this chapter, to point any reader in the direction of one particular class.

That said, there are still many points which you should consider before ever you embark on a course which can lead you to endless delight or an awful lot of expense. The first is: are you really ready to buy your own boat? All right you may well think that you have been bitten by the bug; you have watched those small sailboats dance across the waves and you have managed to get a few trips with a friend. It's great and you can't wait for the next time.

That's good, but it is not really reason enough to dash out and buy a boat. You would do far better to gain some real experience of sailing different types of boats either by joining one of the many clubs which proliferate around the country or by going on a week's course at a sailing school – or both. Just one week at a school will give you the chance to get the feel of sailing different types and will tell you whether or not you have been well and truly bitten by the bug or whether it was merely a nip which shows signs of healing rapidly under lowering clouds and on lurching waves! Apart from the actual physical experience of

sailing you will also have the benefit of the company of hardened sailors who will be able to give you sound advice about the advantages and disadvantages of different classes of boats. They will not all agree, of course, but you should be able to pick up enough knowledge and advice to point you roughly in one direction.

The choice for beginners who want to sail – rather than cruise with an engine – is small in terms of types of boat but very large in classes. The most obvious starting point is a small, lightweight boat with a centerboard. Next comes the ballasted centerboarder which has an integral stub keel and a centerboard which is worked through the keel. This is followed by the keel boat, with a fixed keel (as opposed to the retractable centerboard) with a fin and built-in ballast.

The likelihood is that a young beginner will gain his experience from a small light sailboat and, although there are some *very* small boats with one sail designed with children in mind, it is really best to start in a sloop (two sails) which has enough room for two – a helmsman and crew. One advantage is that the absolute beginner can be accompanied by an experienced instructor at first but can then share his early experiences with another novice so that each learns the importance of working as a team. A second advantage is that the two-sail boat gets you down to the brass tacks of sailing straight away; you are closer to the elements in every respect, low on the water and open to every touch of wind. There is nothing better to teach a novice respect for the elements.

Having decided to buy a boat you can regard the yachting magazines as essential reading for these will give you a clear indication of the wide choice of boats available. A study of the display advertisement pages will reveal illustrations of just about any boat together, very often, with its specification and cost as new, while the classified 'for sale' columns will give you the range of secondhand prices. Such a study will at least enable you to narrow the field somewhat before you set out on your search.

Though I may not be thanked for saying this, it is best, particularly if you are buying your first boat, to go to a recognized yacht broker or boat yard rather than buying privately. The broker will be able to assess your needs if you give him a good idea of your requirements and preferences. In some ways buying a boat, new or secondhand, is like buying a car: it's a good idea to have someone with you who knows what he is talking about. There the similarity ends, particularly where the secondhand boat is concerned, for its value, if it is a good boat, may have appreciated from new whereas that of the secondhand car will have depreciated.

One of the matters to weigh carefully in the

Opposite:
Learning to sail a Wayfarer on England's Hamble River.

Below:
Competitors racing GP 14 sailboats.

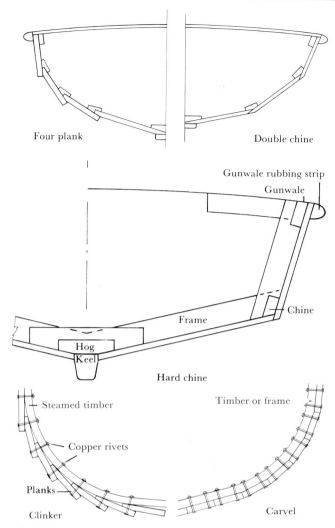

Four plank

Double chine

Gunwale rubbing strip

Gunwale

Frame

Chine

Hog

Keel

Hard chine

Steamed timber

Timber or frame

Copper rivets

Planks

Clinker

Carvel

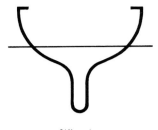

Wineglass

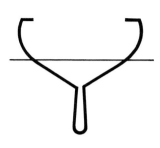

V section

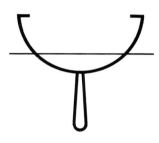

Semi-circular section

IOR hull section

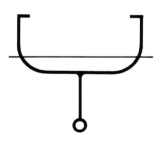

U section

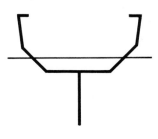

Double chine

that you have the craft thoroughly inspected first. In the case of a small sailboat this can probably be done adequately by an experienced friend but if in doubt and certainly if you are buying anything larger, get a qualified boat surveyor to do the job.

Which do you choose: wood or 'plastic' hull? Now here is a problem for there can be no doubting that a well-maintained wooden-hulled boat is a thing of beauty and a joy if not forever, for as long as it is kept in good condition. Solid wood clinker-built boats in which the hulls are made from separate planks clenched together and each plank overlapping the one below are quite rare these days and tend to be heavy. Far more common is the wooden hull in which the shape of the boat is built up by layers or laminates of timber, each layer lying at a different angle to the one beneath it and bonded to it by waterproof synthetic resin.

An alternative method of wood construction consists of using plywood panels. If two panels are used for each side, one forming the bottom and the other the topsides, this is called a *hard chine* boat. When three panels are used, this is a *double chine*, the chine being the intersection between the sides and/or the bottom. In the latter case there are two sections to the topsides, with one join, and a second join between the lower panel and the bottom – hence 'double chine.' Next comes the *four plank* construction, in which the bottom is a still wider panel and the sides are made up of three narrower planks. The *clinker* has no single-sheet bottom but consists entirely of overlapping planks.

Fiberglass construction can also be from one of several methods which make use of the strength

balance is the fact that in buying a new boat you will be able to get better credit facilities than when buying secondhand – but you will have to buy virtually all the accessories whereas they will – or should – accompany the secondhand craft. However, if you go for a secondhand buy be sure

of glass fiber in its various forms together with its water-resistant properties and inherent stability under extremes of temperature and humidity. Methods of construction include the use of chopped strands of glass fiber held together in 'mats' by a binder; woven rovings which consist of glass fiber strands woven as a cloth; rovings which are untwisted strands; tapes, which are narrow strips of the woven cloth; and tissues, which are very fine versions of the woven cloth.

The most common form in boat building using glass fiber, which is always used in laminates, is the chopped strand mat, though woven rovings are often added for greater impact resistance.

Production which involves large numbers of a particular class very often now employs a male and female (external and internal) mold, the gap between the two giving the thickness of the finished hull. The material used for the hull is placed over the internal mold, mixed with bonding resin and pressed by the external mold under hydraulic pressure. Technologically, the next stage up is the injection molding system in which the material is, as the term suggests, 'injected'

A tempting array of the best in modern design – but down on the ground it can seem quite bewildering!

Contessa yachts being built at J. C. Rogers' yard in Lymington.

between the two master molds. However, the tooling-up of this system is such that it demands a high production run-off to make it economically viable.

A more recent introduction has been the vacuum-forming process using sheets of a thermoplastic. This, too, is strong and forms a very tough shell which presents good resistance to abrasion. However, it does require some form of stiffening either by the use of formers or struts or by using an inner and outer skin with the space between filled with a core of thick polyurethane foam. The completed hull is light but strong and extremely buoyant.

The simplest use of fiberglass is in hand laying-on, which can be done by an individual do-it-yourself man so long as he has a very good, well-finished master mold to work from. This is the method commonly used by hundreds of commercial boat builders for producing hulls, decks and many other components, using molds or patterns which give a highly-polished finish.

The advantage of the fiberglass hull, as we have already said, is that it is virtually maintenance-

An outboard motor is being used to power this Drascombe lugger.

Hobie Cats on the beach at Lanzarote during the World Championships, 1977.

The center hull of Chay Blyth's new 80-foot trimaran takes shape.

Motor sailers under construction. These are Seadog class cruisers being fitted out at the Reg Freeman yard in Southampton. Hull and superstructure is glass fiber.

free whereas perhaps the biggest disadvantage of a wooden hull is that it requires plenty of maintenance to be lavished upon it. However, a really well-maintained wooden hull will appreciate to a greater extent than a 'plastic' hull to the extent that it can, in the long term, become a collector's item.

Whether you are buying a secondhand boat which has a wooden or a fiberglass hull, there are certain basic points you should look for when inspecting the boat. For example, with a fiberglass boat, you should check whether the polyester gel coat has a bright finish or is dull and porous. There may be signs that the hull has begun to delaminate and there will be star crazing marks in the surface where the hull has been struck and possibly weakened.

With a wood hull, check the condition of the woodwork at any points where the paintwork has been chipped or flaked off. Dark patches will indicate damp penetration.

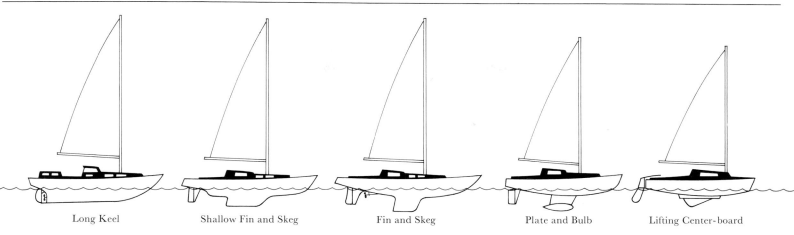

Long Keel   Shallow Fin and Skeg   Fin and Skeg   Plate and Bulb   Lifting Center-board

Make sure that the centerboard case seals are undamaged and watertight and that all buoyancy compartments are sound. Do not be afraid to use a bit of strength in checking that fixtures and fittings are generally sound. Inspect all screws carefully and watch out for rust stains. Similarly, look for corrosion and wear on fittings such as cleats, sheaves, on rigging and at the foot of the mast. Are the mast, boom, tiller and all spars clean and straight and do the sails show signs of chafe, thinness, threadbare patches or general dirtiness?

One danger which inexperienced purchasers face in buying their first boat from new without proper guidance is that they may well go for a boat which appears to suit their requirements perfectly but which proves to be a completely new and untried class. It may give you a certain feeling

Building a Moth hard-chine sailboat from a kit in a garage.

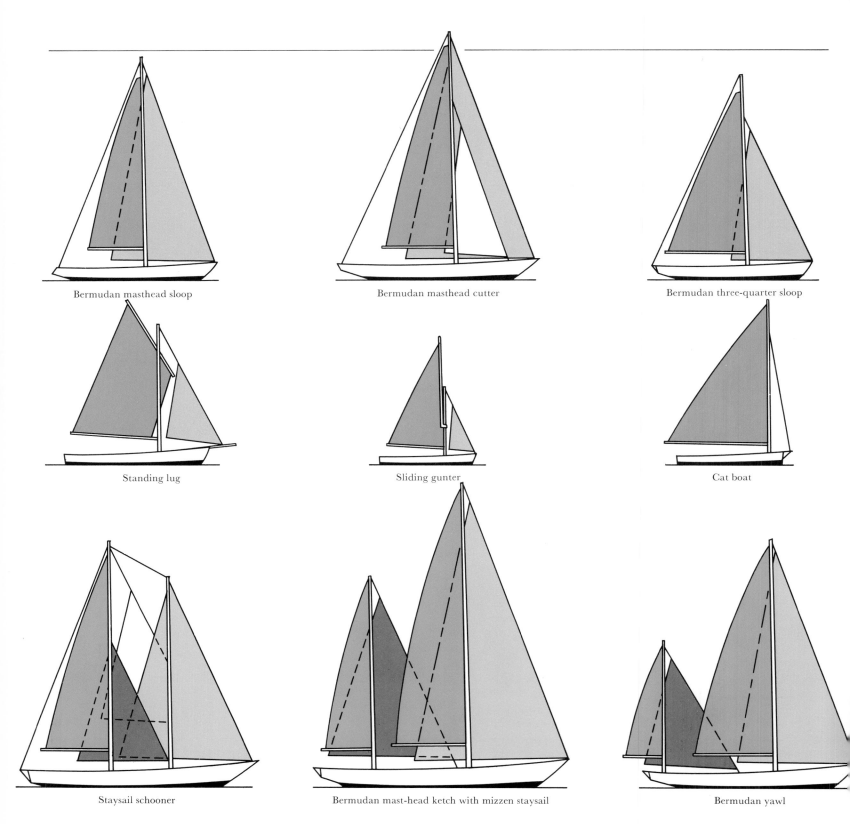

Bermudan masthead sloop

Bermudan masthead cutter

Bermudan three-quarter sloop

Standing lug

Sliding gunter

Cat boat

Staysail schooner

Bermudan mast-head ketch with mizzen staysail

Bermudan yawl

of exclusiveness to have one of only a few but it is far better to go for a long-running design. By all means, keep your eye out for news of that new design's progress and, if it survives the test of time, think again about buying it. Unfortunately, each season sees the emergence of a number of new designs but the great majority sink without trace – not literally but in the sense that they exhibit some inherent weakness of design or manufacture or simply do not find a market.

If you are tempted to buy a boat of untried design and then wish to dispose of it, either because it is not satisfactory or because you want to move on to something larger, you could find that your boat has virtually no resale value.

All the foregoing applies just as much to yachts and motorcruisers as it does to the smaller sail-boats. However, if you are looking for a large boat your task will be that much more difficult – in proportion, really, to the extra amount you will be spending – and there will be a need to go into even greater detail before committing yourself. Gather together as much illustrated literature as you can which deals with the type of boat for which you are looking and read the brochures and pamphlets with care. In particular, do not

The Timpenny 670, an easily transported family boat.

A Finnish-built Nauticat 44 on trials in the Solent. A solidly built ocean-going motor/sailer providing spacious accommodation and good all-round performance.

be misled by some of the wording, which tends for example, to turn a pokey galley into a spacious one and make everything sound idyllic. Nor should you be taken in by photographs of interiors: clever use of the right lenses and lighting can turn a cabin into a ballroom! Always check the specification to make sure that what *looks* like a 8ft (2.4m) width is not really only 6ft 6in (1.9m). Be careful that in your natural desire to buy a boat into which you, your wife and two children can all fit, you do not think that because the boat you are reading about has four berths, it will have plenty of room. If it's an 18-footer, for example, you will find living and sleeping accommodation is pretty cramped.

You will, presumably, have decided whether you want to go for real sailing, in which case you will be looking for a yacht with an auxiliary engine, or for 'motor-sailing,' which means that the engine will be of more importance than the sails, or for pure motor-cruising, which involves no sails at all. The latter does not really concern us here, except to say that those who are content with this form of life on the water can still learn a lot by reading a few sailing books. The 'motor-sailer' tends to be a more spacious type of boat offering greater comfort in its fixtures and fittings but not performing as well under sail as the yacht with an auxiliary motor which is started up only as secondary assistance rather than as a primary source of propulsion.

Again, it is all a matter of personal preference backed by professional advice and supported by your bank account. The cost does not end once you have bought the boat: maintenance will eat into your pocket and you will need to weigh this in the balance too.

Finally, whatever your final choice may be, please do not forget to insure the boat *and* its ancillary equipment – not just for your own sake but also for the sake of those who will be sharing the water with you.

Good sailing.

Admiral's Cup, *56, 157*
Admiralty List of Lights and Tide Tables, 134
Admiralty Pilots, 134
Aerodynamic force, 23, 29, 97, 117, 120
Aerofoil, 84
Air mass tracks, *149*
Air tanks, 41
America's Cup races, 12-13
Anchor, 56, 60, 70, 106, 110, *137-38,*
　164-65; buoy, 56; chain, 56, 70;
　Danforth, *137;* Fisherman's, 56, *137;*
　Grapnel, 56; Kedge, 56; line, 56; Plow,
　56, *137;* Sea, 160, 164-65
Anchoring, 136, 138, *138*
Anticyclone, 152-53
Automatic pilot, 74

Bailers, 60, 78
Bailing, 105-106
Ballast, 23, *24*, 38
Barge, *11*
Barograph, 153
Barometer, 130, 153-54, 160
Battens, 48
Beam, 24; Beam on, 81, 98; reaching, 81-2,
　84
Bear away, 29, 96
Bearings, 128-43; Diagram, *133;* Magnetic,
　128, 141; Relative, 128; True, 128, 141
Beaufort scale, 60-61, 150, 154, *154*
Bermuda cutter, *114-15, 188*
Bermuda rig, *47*
Bilges, 177
Binnacle, 128
Bitt, 70
Block and tackle system, 53
Blocks, *36,* 37, 48-50, *53,* 178
Boat show, *180*
Bollard, 169-70
Bolt line, 48; ropes, 46-7; track, 55
Boom, 32, *32,* 34, *36,* 45, 47-9, 53, 75, 86,
　96-7, 122, 124, 162-63
Bosun's chair, *173*
Bow, 12, 32, *32,* 34, 45-6, 81-2, 98, 104,
　125, 142, 161, 164-65
Bridle, 49
Brixham trawler, *178*
Broaching to, 86, 93, 161
Bulb, *187*
Buoyancy, 23, *24,* 38, 41, 60, 110; aids, *58,*
　64, *64,* 105, 108; compartments, 187
Buoys, *64, 66,* 67-8, *67,* 70; cardinal system,
　67; Dan, *64;* Horseshoe, *64;* lateral
　system, 67; mooring, 68, 70; pick-up, 70
Burgee, 32, *32*

Capsizing, 41, 46, 86, 88, 93, 98, *100-101,*
　102-13, *104-107*
Casting off, 78-97
Catamaran, *49, 103*

Cat boat, *188*
Centerboard, *passim;* case, 187; lifting, *187;*
　sailboat, *32,* 182
Center of effort (CE), 29, 117, 120, 124
Cervantes Trophy Race, *145*
Charts, 62, 130, 133-34, *133,* 138-42;
　actual distance, 139; chart distance, 139;
　coastal, 134; datum, 134
Cleat, 32, 34, 37, 45-6, 49, 52-3, *53, 87,* 88,
　96, *110,* 165, *169*
Clew, 46-50, *48,* 86, 88, 94, *163;* cringle, 48
Close-hauled course, 32, 36, 82, *83,* 84,
　93-4, *95, 96,* 116, *116,* 124
Cloud formations, 152, *152;* cirrus, *153,*
　160; cumulus, *154-55*
Coast Pilots of the Oceanographic Office, 134
Cockpit, 37, 46, 48-9
Collision, 72, *72,* 74; *Rules for the Prevention*
　of Collision at Sea, 73
Compass, *37,* 128-30, 140-42; bowl, 128;
　card, 128; domed, 128; grid steering,
　128; hand-bearing, 128, *129,* 141;
　magnetic influence on, 129; porthole
　type, *128;* rose, 140-41, *140;* traditional,
　128
Corrosion, 174, 187
Course, 141
Cowes, 68
Craning out, *175*
Crosstrees (spreaders), 32, *32,* 46, 48, 52,
　120
Cruiser, *156*
Cruiser/racer, *33*
Cunningham Hole, *45,* 53, *54*
Current, 133
Cutters, 12, *166-67, 188*

Datum line, 134
Davies, Paul, *44*
Dead ahead, 82
Dead before the wind, 82, 85, 93, 96
Depressions, 152-53, 155
Dinghies, *20,* 160
Dismasting, *158,* 177
Displacement, 24
Downhaul, *48,* 49, 52, 54, 88, 122
Draft, 136
Drag, 24-5, 27; wave drag, 25, 27
Drowning, 65

European Championships, *27*

Fairlead, 46, 49-51, 56, 106
Fiberglass hull, *172,* 174
Fin, 182, *187*
Fore-and-aft (helm amidships), 81-2
Fore-and-aft sail (lateen), 8, 34, *47*
Foresail, *17*
Forestay, 32, *32,* 34, 45-6, 50, 52, 78-9, 88,
　89, 98

Francis, Clare, *17*
Friction, 27
Full-and-by, 70, 82, *83,* 84, *84,* 99

Gaff rig, *46*
Gimbals (gymbals), 128
Globe, 138-39, *139*
Going about, 93, 95
Gooseneck, *32,* 34, 45, 47-8, 53, *54,* 162
Goosewinging, 85, 99
Greenwich meridian, 138-40
Gunter, Sliding, *188*
Gunwale, 40-41, *41,* 81, 94-5, 103-104, 106
Guy, 48, 52, *48, 87,* 88, 97
Gybing, 86, *86-7,* 93-8, *94, 98,* 161

Halyard, *passim*
Hanks, 46, 160
Harness, 40-41, 160
Head board, 47-8, 88
Head on, 72
Headsails, 47, 96, *122,* 164, *169*
Head to wind, *83,* 95
Heaving-to, 164
Heeling, 81-2, 84, 94, 103, 117, 122, 125
Helm, 82, 86, 103
Helmsman, *passim*
Horse, *36,* 37-8, 45, 53
Hull, 12, 23-5, *24,* 27-8, 41, 44-5, 82, 85,
　105-106, 108, 125, 133; Carvel, *183;*
　Chine, 183, *183, 187;* Clinker, 183, *183;*
　Fiberglass, *172,* 174, 178, 183-86, *186;*
　Four plank, 183, *183;* Metal, 178;
　Plywood, 178; Wooden, 175-76, 183, 186
Hydrodynamic force, 29, 37, 117
Hydrographic Department *Notices to*
　Mariners, 140
Hydrostatic pressure, 23, 38
Hypothermia, 64

Isobars, 152, *152*

Jib, *passim*
John Player World Speed Trials, *103*

Keel, 23, *23,* 24, 81, 88, 93, 182; Bulb, 24;
　even, 81, 88, 93; Fin, 24; Stub, 182
Keel boat, 23, 28, *122,* 182, *187*
Kicking strap (Vang), 32, 34, *34, 36,* 45-6,
　45, 48, 53, 60, 75, 86, 93-4, 97, *120,* 124,
　162
Knots, 50-51, 54, 56, 168-71, *168-71*

Laminar flow, 23, *23,* 28, 84
Landmarks, 133-34, 141-42
Lateen, *see* fore-and-aft
Lateral Resistance, 23, *23,* 24; center of
　(CLR), 117, 120
Lateral trim, 81-2
Laying-up, 174-79

Leadline, 130, 136
Leaning out, 85
Leech, *48*, 49, 120, *162–63*
Lee helm, 29, 116, 120; shroud, 84
Leeward, 29, 81, 85–6, *85*, *87*, 103, 106, *124*, 125, 128, 165
Leeway, 23, 37, 84–5, 141, 164
Life jacket, 64, 74, 105, 108
Lifeline harness, *62*, 74, *158*, 160
Life raft, 160
Log, 130, 133
Longitudinal trim, 82
Luff, luffing, *passim*
Lugg, *48*, *188*
Lugger, *85*
Lugsail, *46*

McDonald-Smith, I, *88*
Mainsail, *passim*
Maintenance, 174–79, *176*, *178–79*, 189; Engine, 179; Painting, *174*, *175–76*
Man overboard procedure, 74
Mast, *passim*
Masthead lights, *74–5*
Measuring equipment, 130
Mercator's Projection, 136
Mooring, *99*
Motor cruiser, *188–89*
Motor sailer, *186*, 189
Musto, Keith, *30*

National Weather Service (U.S.), 146, 148
Navigation, 133, 139–40, 142–43; equipment, 130, *130*, 133
Navigator, 134

Offshore, 136, 142
Offshore cruiser/racer, *33*

Pagot brothers, *41*
Pattison, Rodney, *85*
Physical fitness, 110–11, *111*, 113; Exercises, 113
Planing, 27, 82, *82*, *89*, 117
Port, 28, 46, 72, 78, 81, *83*, 128, 142
Pressure, 152, *152*

Racing, 12
Radar, 146, *146*
Radio, 130, 146; Radio Direction Finder (RDF), *146*
Reaching, 36, *51*, 52, 82, *82–5*, 84, 86, 97–8
Reed's Almanac, 134
Reefing, 53, 162–64; roller, *162–63*; slab, *160*, *162–63*
Renseignements Relatifs aux Documents Nautique et à la Navigation, 134
Resuscitation, 65–7
Rigging, 8, 12, 44–56, 60, *175*, *177*; diagrams, *45–7*; fore-and-aft, 12, *46*;

Gunter, *46*; running, 44, 50, 52; square, 12, *46*; standing, 44, 50, 52
Ropes, 50–51, 54, 56, 168–71, *168–71*, 174; coiling, 168; knotting, 50–51, 54, 56, 168–71, *168–71*; mooring, 168; splicing, *168–71*; whipping, *170–71*
Rudder, *passim*
Running, 82, *83*, 93, 136, 160–65; aground, 136; before the storm, *164–65*; clean before the wind, 93; free, *160–61*, 164

Sailing: safety, 60–75, *64*, *158*, 160–65; single-handed, 111; theory, 21–9, *22–5*, *116–17*
Sails, *passim*
Schooner, 12, *188*
Sextant, 130, *130*
Shackle, 34, 46–7, *53*, 54, 56, 79
Shoring-up, *174*
Shrouds, *passim*
Sitting out, 60, 125
Simmonds, Colin, *88*
Skeg, *187*
Sloop, *158*, *182*, *188*
Soundings, 134
Sparkman & Stephens, 12–13
Spinnakers, *passim*
Spreaders, *see* Crosstrees
Spritsails, *47*
Square-riggers, *11*
Stability, 60
Starboard, 28, 46, 72, *72*, 78, 81, *83*, 128, 142
Staysails, *46–7*
Stern, 82, 98, 112, 165
Sternway, 117, 165
Storms, *158*, 160–65; eye of, 155

Tack, *passim*
Tidal stream, *137*, 141, *141*
Tide, 60, 133–34, 136, *136*, 138, 141
Tiller, *passim*
Toe straps, *37*, 38, 40, 111, 113
Topping lift, 49, 52, 88, 162
Training ships, 8, *11*
Transit, *141*, 142
Transom, *81*, 82, 95, *105–106*
Trapeze, 38, 40–41, *41*, 81, 98, 111, 113
Trim, 93–4, *124–25*; fore-and-aft, 125; lateral, 125
Trimaran, *186*
Tuning, 116–25, *118*
Turbulence, 23, *23*, 28, 82, 84
Turner, Ted, 13
12-Meter yacht, 12–13

Uphaul, *48*

Valentin, Johan, 12
Vang, *see* kicking strap

Warp, 160, 165, *165*
Waves, 25, 27–8, 60, 96, 98
Weather, 60, 62, 146–63, *146*; forecast, 60, 140, 146–55, *151*, 160
Weather helm, 29, 32, 116–17, *116–17*, 120, 125
Wet suit, *58*, 62, 64
Wetted area, 25, 27, 81–2, 125
Whitbread round the world race, *17*
Wind, 22–3, *23*, 28, 36, 46, 54, 60–62, *65*, 82, 84, 86, 94, 96, 106, 124–25, 148–55, *152*, 164, *164*, 174
Windsurfing, *62*
Windward, 52, 81, 84, *85*, 86, *87*, *106–107*, 122, 128, 160, 163, 165
Woodison, Johnson, *44*

Yacht, 12, *188–89*
Yaw, 37, 93

BOATS

ADC Accutrac, *17*
America, 12, *15*
America replica, *15*
Amerigo Vespucci, *8*
Australia, 12–13, *18*

Ballyhoo, *145*
Battlecry, *15*
Bumblebee, *64*

Cherub, *96*, *117*
Columbia, 12–13
Constellation, 12
Contessa, *184*
Courageous, 12–13
Crossbow I, *25*

Dame Pattie, 12
Dar Pormoza, *8*

Elka, *127*
Enterprise, 13
Etchells 22, *120*

Finn, *101–102*
Fireball, *89*
Flying Dutchman, *20*, *30*, *41*, 44, *51*, *85*
France, 12
France I, 13
France II, 13
France III, 13
Freedom, *18*, 40, *114–15*, 122

Genoa, *17*
Gretel, 12
Gretel II, 12

INDEX

Heath's Condor, 110, 179
Hobie Cat, 113, 185
Hornet, 104

Incisif, 68
Intrepid, 12
Ismana, 162

Kruzenshtern, 8

Laser, 93, 108, 117, 125
Lazy E, 41
Lionheart, 13, 13

Marionette, 6
Mayflower, 8
Merlin Rocket, 81
Midnight Sun, 91

Moody 39, 127
Moth, 187

Nacra, 103
Nauticat 44, 189

OK, 84
Old Gaffers, 10

Phantom, 28-9, 82

Red Rock, 15
Rubin, 64

Saudade, 62
Sceptre, 12
Sea-Dog, 186
Shearwater, 49

Skibberean, 143
Skipper, 181
Soling, 27, 34, 39, 50, 79, 88, 92-3, 98
Southern Cross, 12
Sovereign, 12
Star, 124
Sverige, 13

Timpenny 670, 189
Tovarishch, 8

Uin-Na-Maru, 56

Weatherly, 12
Williwaw, 56

470, 37
505, 27, 37

The publishers would like to thank the following for their kind assistance and for supplying the 200 illustrations:

Yachting World, Yachts and Yachting, John Watney, Colin Jarman, Ajax News Photos, Douglas West Ltd, Bill Banks, The French Government Tourist Office, Robert O'Neill Photography, Tabur Marine (GB) Ltd, David Kernahan, François Richard, K.H. Publicity Ltd, Paul Wright, David Forster, Laurence Bradbury, Baumann of Hilterfingen, Jeffrey J. Smorley.

Special thanks are also due to Ken Smith who drew all the line illustrations and the Controller of Her Majesty's Stationery Office for kind permission to reproduce the charts which appear on pp 135, pp 136 and pp 137.